JOHNNY RAPID
EXPOSED

HOW THE STAR TRIUMPHED OVER HIS PAST

JOHNNY RAPID

JOHNNY RAPID

---•••◆•••---

JOHNNY
RAPID
EXPOSED

---•••◆•••---

HOW THE STAR TRIUMPHED
OVER HIS PAST

ISBN: 978-1-953282-09-5

Nonfiction > Biography & Autobiography > Rich & Famous
Nonfiction > Biography & Autobiography > Entertainment & Performing Arts

REBELL BOOKS
Atlanta GA
Printed in the United States

RebellBooks.com

TABLE OF CONTENTS

———•··◆··•———

DEDICATION

———•··◆··•———

Easily enough, this book is dedicated to the models I've had the pleasure of working with, fans with their continued loyalty and support, and to Tee Gates, a man of pure heart!

ACKNOWLEDGEMENT

———·••◆••·———

It is imperative that I mention the many companies that have helped make me the star I am today, for without them Johnny Rapid would still be dormant, only existing within my dreams. Here are those companies in chronological order.

- Edward James
- Cashmodels
- Bukkakeboys
- Boysfirsttime
- Men.com
- Cybersocket
- TLAVideo
- AEBN
- Fleshjack
- Mindgeek
- Pornhub
- Onlyfans
- Nakedsword
- NMG
- Streamate

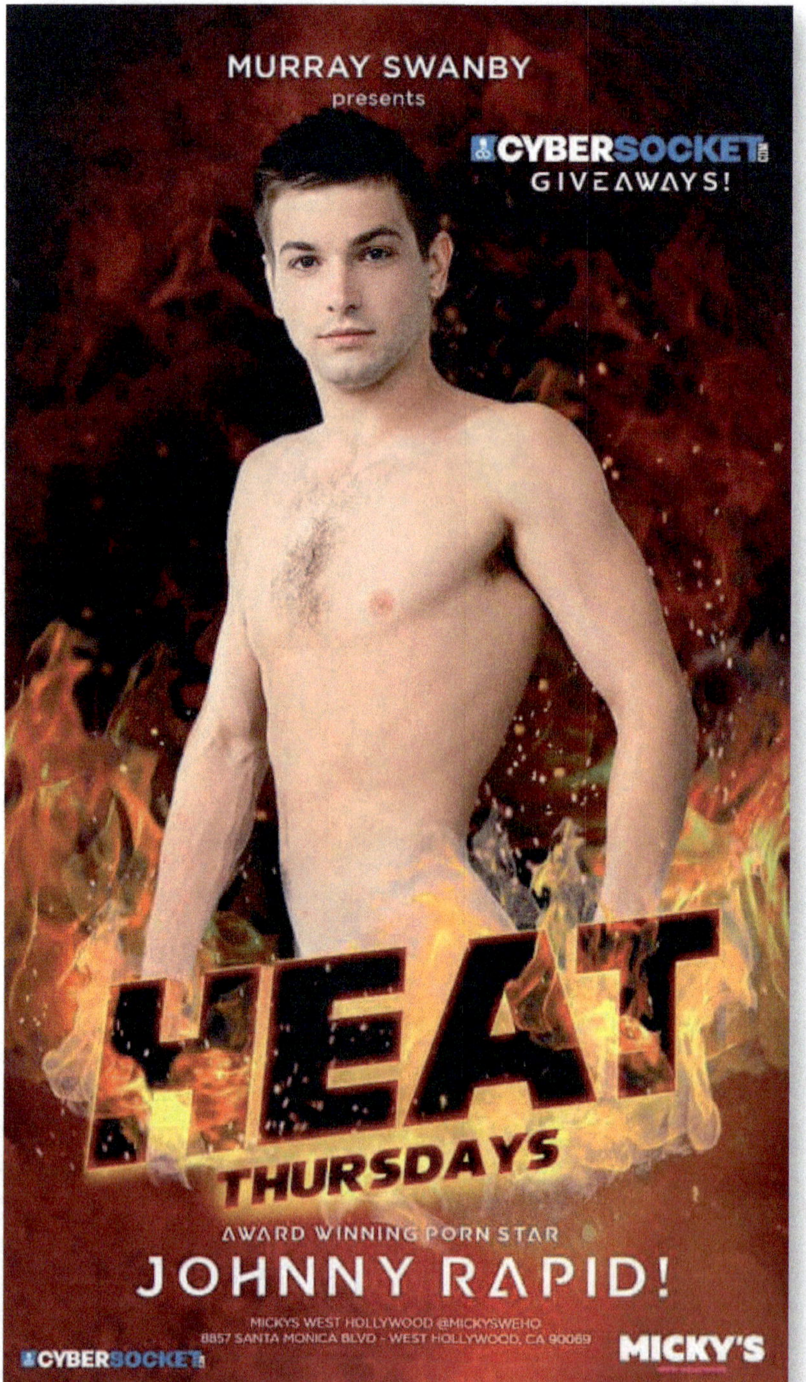
MURRAY SWANBY
presents
CYBERSOCKET
GIVEAWAYS!
HEAT
THURSDAYS
AWARD WINNING PORN STAR
JOHNNY RAPID!
MICKYS WEST HOLLYWOOD @MICKYSWEHO
8857 SANTA MONICA BLVD - WEST HOLLYWOOD, CA 90069
CYBERSOCKET
MICKY'S

Who is Johnny Rapid?

PROLOGUE

————◆•••◆————

"After all the years of torment and harassment, I, Johnny Rapid, finally control my life!"

"Never in my wildest dreams could I have expected to be standing on this stage accepting the highest award in the industry," thought Hylan to himself. 2011 had been very good to him. It had been a great year!

There he was, holding a silver statuette depicting a man reaching for the sky with upstretched arms. Hylan Taylor, better known by his trade name, *Johnny Rapid*, could not have been more thrilled. It was almost as if time was standing still for him. His mind was flashing back and forth between his past and what his future held in store. It was *his* time. The crowd was roaring in delight as their newfound hero held his award high over his head as he profusely thanked his adoring fans.

Hylan had indeed become Johnny Rapid. They were now one.

To make things even more amazing, he almost turned down the invitation to attend the ceremony.

Thinking back to earlier in the day, Hylan remembered contemplating his friend's request to attend the Cybersocket Awards that evening. "Do you think it's worth our time to go?" asked Hylan. "This is my first time in Hollywood, and for that matter, California. I don't want to waste time when we could be doing some serious exploring if you know what I mean."

Hylan had traveled to California from his native Georgia with his buddy, who went by the nickname, *Yah-Know*. They had met at a gay bar in Atlanta just a few months earlier. Hylan always laughed to himself over his friend's odd name. After years of teasing, Yah-Know finally accepted that all of his friends had decided to address him as *Yah-Know* because of his annoying habit of seemingly starting every sentence with, well, you guessed it, "You know!"

"You know, we can party anytime," said Yah-Know. "This is L.A. Life goes on here 24/7. I say, we go. After all, it can only help grow our connections with the in-crowd. Plus, we'll probably be able to hang with some people who can take us to all the best places."

"His buddy was right," thought Hylan to himself. One never knew who you might run into at a club. The Cybersocket Awards would be packed with important people. If he wanted to continue his climb to the top, attending the awards ceremony could only help.

Hyland and his buddy were in Hollywood to shoot a pilot for a TV show. The producers were looking for a twist to the tired, old dramas playing throughout network programming. It was now the year 2012. The director wanted to shake things up with a series about a delinquent screw-up becoming a superhero. Hylan's rise as a star and innate intelligence made him a perfect fit for the role.

Not only was this Hylan's first trip to the west coast, but it was also his first time on an airplane. Despite all the hassles they encountered at the airport, Hylan was still on a high just from the excitement of travel.

"Okay," said Hylan. "Let's go!" Hylan was feeling invincible. He was now truly living life in his *superhero* mode. He believed that his transformation into Johnny Rapid was now genuinely complete.

Suddenly, his mind flashed back to the present. Hylan, as Johnny Rapid, had just accepted the highest award in the industry. There he stood in awe. He had arrived as Johnny Rapid and now believed that his career would soar. Then, without an additional thought or regret, he reverted back to Hylan Taylor and began to cry.

Hylan thought to himself, "It was nice to be seen, to feel accomplished. So many people were against me and told me I was shit. But that night, I felt seen. I felt appreciated! For maybe the first time in his life. Johnny Rapid and Hylan Taylor were not just one but could now exist together.

Or, at least, that's what he thought.

•••◆•••

The Cybersocket Awards ceremony had catapulted Johnny Rapid's prospects to near-stellar limits. Hylan now found himself in such demand that he regretted signing the somewhat restrictive contract just a few months earlier.

The contract did not set limitations on his performances and co-stars as much as it did on the percentage of profits he received. Hylan did not understand just how little control he had over his career until an incredibly lucrative opportunity arose.

And what was this opportunity? It was the stunning possibility of performing with Justin Bieber.

In some ways, Johnny Rapid and Justin Bieber's success tracks had a lot in common. They both started their careers at about the same time. Because of their young ages, both artists found themselves pawns in other people's bigger plans. Although the two young men were in very different entertainment fields, they had in common the private torment of trying to figure out just who they really were deep down inside. All of this while trying to maintain a positive image for their fans.

In early 2015, just a few short years into their careers, MEN.com approached Justin Bieber with a $2.0 million proposal. This was shortly after the famous Justin Bieber kiss that caused the world to speculate on his sexuality. Bieber was offered the enormous sum of money to perform a scene with Johnny Rapid to take advantage of Bieber's and Johnny Rapid's notoriety.

When Hylan was told of the opportunity for his Johnny Rapid persona, his first thought was, "How much do I get?"

The marketing and distribution opportunities would be enormous. The profits huge. Johnny Rapid was already a star at the pinnacle of his profession. However, this one thirty-minute scene would vault him to number one!

Yet, Hylan wanted more.

His contract dictated that his manager had sole control over what he did professionally and what percentage Johnny Rapid received from his endeavors. When Hylan was told that he would get $1/8^{th}$ of the amount being offered to Justin Bieber, he demanded more. "After all, shouldn't the lion's share of the profits go to the performers?" Well, that's what Hylan thought. But, it wasn't until that incident that he learned the hard way that Johnny Rapid was just a component, just a tool, in his manager's bag of tricks.

Hylan realized at that moment his limitations as Johnny Rapid. His mind drifted back to his teenage years when he lived in a constant state of mental torment. What was the future going to hold for Hylan Taylor? Was he destined to allow *Johnny Rapid* to become his entire life? Should he take a stand and demand more, or just use each opportunity presented as a stepping stone toward future success?

Hylan asked himself, "What would Johnny Rapid do?" After all, hadn't he truly become *Johnny Rapid*?

His thoughts returned to his past, and he reflected on how he had reached this point in his life. Would this be just a turning point? Were his limitations self-imposed, or were others directing his future?

Who is Johnny Rapid?

PART I.
THE EARLY YEARS

CHAPTER 1.
TRAGEDY AND A NEW BEGINNING

———•••◆•••———

Life had not been easy for Hylan Taylor. Just about anything that could have gone wrong seemingly did. He started to contemplate one of the most critical years in his life.

For most of us, adversity is just a part of life. We all have to deal with life's difficulties. It is a rare exception that an individual can have a perfect childhood and grow up to become a so-called average member of society. Adversity and challenges build character, right?

Well, for Hylan Taylor, a scared fifth-grader, adversity forced him to retreat into his dreams. In these dreams, his subconscious created Johnny Rapid, his superhero. And Johnny Rapid was not just a super-hero *to* Hylan Taylor. He was Hylan Taylor *as* a superhero.

Yet, unlike most people who allow their trials and tribulations to wreak havoc on their future. Hylan made his dreams and Johnny Rapid become a reality. He turned his challenges into accomplishments, his dreams into reality, and his fears became the basis of his strength.

But, it certainly wasn't as easy as it sounds.

•◆•

His fifth-grade year could have been turned into a horror movie used to scare any kid into finishing their homework or eating that god-awful broccoli.

At the tender age of ten, Hylan was pretty much your typical kid dealing with the usual anxieties that came with elementary school. As with most kids that age, he was unaware of the life-changing events happening around him. Like most parents, Hylan's Mom and Dad chose to shelter him from the day-to-day issues that piled up and began to plague his family's life.

The first shock to Hylan's existence was his father going to prison. Hylan had no idea that his father was in so much trouble. After all, his dad had always been there for him. Like many kids with strict parents, Hylan grew to wish he wasn't around so much. When he was told that his dad wasn't coming home… *ever*, he started to blame himself for sometimes wishing the worst for his troubled father.

Shortly afterward, Hylan learned that his grandfather had disappeared. He was shocked to discover that his granddad was cheating on his grandmother. To make matters worse, his grandparents divorced not just over the cheating but because of his beloved granddad's drinking problem. When his grandpa visited, he portrayed himself as a friend and mentor, only to disappear without saying goodbye. Within weeks, Hylan had lost his only two male role models. He started to wonder if somehow any of this was his fault.

In many ways, Hylan would miss his dad the most. There was a positivity that permeated their relationship and that made their time together a great pleasure. Hylan looked up to his dad as a gentle giant. Now, Hylan's life would be missing an important piece, like a car without its steering wheel.

Well, at least young Hylan still had his home. His mom was determined to do her best for her son. She was a buyer for a large manufacturing company. She was successful and brought home her talent for organization and discipline. He knew he could count on his mom. Hylan was a bright child and enjoyed school. He loved to learn and expand his knowledge. His mother went out of her way to ensure he had the tools and direction to do well.

Without warning… A fire destroyed everything he had. After returning from school one day, he was confronted by the devastation. His home was a charred cinder. Everything he had and looked forward to enjoying was gone.

Hylan and his mom found themselves in an old camper living off of the generosity of a local church. Eventually, they found a place to live in a nearby community forcing Hylan to start over in a new school.

Hylan had lost everything he associated with home and school in what seemed like a blink of an eye. It wasn't fair. He had to start all over with just the things he could carry. His mom was overwhelmed but still tried to push on. However, their recent life challenges were also taking a daunting toll on her.

As if life couldn't get any worse, his new school turned out to be an earthly purgatory, a place of no acceptance and safety. Hylan's only escape was when he could turn off his daytime nightmare to retreat to his dream world. This nocturnal fantasy place would lead him to his future as Johnny Rapid.

•◆•

Imagine being just ten years old and starting completely over.

Hylan felt as if he had nobody but his mom for support. Although, within a matter of months, his mom had a new man in her life, Hylan was unsure and uncomfortable around him. And, even with this new man in her life, his mom was still a wreck doing her best to maintain a cheerful face for her troubled son.

Much to his dismay, Hylan's new school enrollment landed in the middle of the semester. In almost all ways, Hylan felt like an outsider.

Although very bright, Hylan was small for his age. He became easy fodder for the school bullies and a target for the in-crowd to ridicule. With no place else to go, his only escape, his only solace came from retreating to his bedroom to sleep.

Like most kids, Hylan had an active imagination. He also was blessed with the ability to remember most, if not all, of his nighttime dreams. His dreams were so vivid that Hylan sometimes had difficulty separating his fantasies from reality. In a way, he wanted them to be real. While Hylan was bullied and picked on in school, he was relaxed and enjoyed life in his dreams. The only disappointing part of his dreams was that he was always alone. He wanted to be with other kids. He wanted to make friends and enjoy playing with others again.

Hylan was asleep and dreaming one night. When, to his amazement and delight, a kindly gentleman appeared and gave him a gift. In his dream, Hylan was sitting in a chair. It was almost as if the chair was somehow hovering within a cloud. Reaching down to Hyland, the man handed Hylan a bright red belt with a yellow and blue buckle. Hylan was mesmerized by the gift. When he finally looked up, he saw the man turn and walk away. The gentleman's face was a blur, and his body seemed to melt away like a morning fog fading in favor of the bright, sunlit sky.

Staring at the belt, Hylan stood and did the only thing that occurred to him. He put it on.

Dreams can be funny things. They are always unique to the individual and can, for whatever reason, become confusing. Some dreams can cause happiness. Others can create abject terror. In this case, both feelings collided to give Hylan an emotional rollercoaster that changed his life forever. When he put on the belt, he became Johnny Rapid.

CHAPTER 2.

THE BELT

———•··◆··•———

The initial experience of wrapping the belt around his waist and buckling it together was shocking... *literally*! Hylan struggled to understand why it felt like he was being stabbed by thousands of needles that seemed to bond to his nerves. Only after what seemed like an eternity, which had actually only been about 15 seconds, did the odd tingling cease, and everything around him changed.

The chair and the surrounding cloud disappeared. It was replaced with a windowless, all-white room. The only object in the room was a freestanding, beveled-edged mirror that looked as if it belonged in the bedroom of a Victorian lady. It was oval and stood over six-feet high. The wood trim and decorative carvings typically would have drawn the user's eyes to admire the beauty of the frame if not for what Hylan saw in its reflection. He was cloaked in a skintight yellow and blue costume, highlighted by his newly acquired *red belt*.

The painful chore of putting on the belt had turned into an almost sensual warmth that filled his entire body with strength and fortitude. Taking a traditional Superman stance, Hylan admired his new look. But that wasn't all.

When Hylan started to think about what had happened to him, he realized that he had become somebody else. He was not looking at Hylan Taylor anymore. He was looking at Johnny Rapid, a superhero. For the first time since he could remember, Hylan felt confident and strong. Jumping up and shifting his weight from one foot to the other, he started to enjoy his newfound power.

Suddenly, he was awakened by his mother shaking him. She said, "Hylan, honey. It's time to get up and get ready for school. I have to get you to the bus so that I can go to work." After making sure her son was getting dressed, she turned and left his bedroom.

Hylan was mortified. Although he tended to remember most of his dreams, he had never enjoyed one that seemed so very, very real. His disappointment was palpable. His fear of returning to school was overwhelming.

"I don't want to go to school," mumbled Hylan. However, he knew from experience that come hell or high water; he had to go. There was no way his mom could stay home. Hylan had to get dressed and chase down that stupid yellow bus.

Yet, this day was not like the others that had only brought misery and sometimes pain. Unlike past times, Hylan couldn't quite shake the feeling that this day had brought a new beginning. Smiling to himself, Hylan got dressed, loaded up his backpack, and almost marched into the kitchen.

His mom handed him a paper bag containing a sandwich, a banana, and some crackers for his lunch. She almost pushed him out the front door, following her son out. Hylan's mom knew that it was always an annoying game between Hylan and the bus driver, Julie. Julie had a strict rule that you had to be waiting contritely to be picked up or find another way to get one's butt to school.

Hylan made it to the bus stop just as the bus appeared. He got on and took his usual spot just behind the driver. Sitting back in his seat, he started to contemplate his dream and just who Johnny Rapid was.

His thoughts returned to the yellow and blue costume with the incredible bright red belt buckle. What was this all about? Even more concerning to him was, "Who is Johnny Rapid?" The name had just appeared in his mind as if the character had always existed. "Wait a minute! I am Johnny Rapid," said Hylan to himself. "I am the super-hero!" He did not realize that he was thinking out loud. Julie looked up and stared at Hylan in her rearview mirror with a look of horror. Something was going on.

A fight had broken out in the back of the bus. Two older students were duking it out over something to do with a small red bag.

The bus driver looked back over her shoulder and said, "If you're such a superhero, can you do something about that fight?"

Without thinking, Hylan stood up and made his way to the back of the bus. The kids near the combatants were taking sides and rooting for their favorite. Hylan could feel the warm tingle he had enjoyed during his dream. He felt as if he could do anything. *Nothing* could stop him from doing the right thing.

With one hand, Hylan grabbed the shoulder of the bigger teen and pushed him back into his seat. With the other hand, he grabbed the smaller guy, held him up over his head, and said, "This fight is over! Take your problems somewhere else, not on this bus."

The two larger teens stared at Hylan in awe. They jumped up like two caged Pit Bulls raring for a fight. As they both reached for Hylan, they found themselves pushed back into their seats by an unknown force. "Hey!" said the obnoxious prick that had tormented Hylan in the past. "What the hell are you doing?" He tried to get up and, in a flash, discovered that he was stuck in his seat.

Hylan turned to the second guy and said, "The bus driver asked me to stop the fight. If you want to continue, wait until you get to school."

Looking shocked, the two bullies attempted to rise. They couldn't. It was as if they were wearing invisible seatbelts that secured them to their seats. The two combatants looked at each other, then back at Hylan. There was something different about the kid they used to bully.

Hylan turned and started to walk back to the front of the bus. As he did, one girl began to clap, then two. In just seconds, the entire bus was clapping and cheering!

When Hylan returned to the front of the bus and sat down, the bus driver turned again and said, "Thanks for taking care of that. You did good, kid! *And*, I like your new outfit."

Hylan said, "What outfit?" At that moment, he looked down. The red buckle was almost glowing. It was tightly wrapped around his yellow and blue costume. He had become Johnny Rapid!

Suddenly, the roosters started crowing, his eyes opened, and there he was… still in bed.

CHAPTER 3.
WAS IT JUST A DREAM?

Have you ever suddenly awakened from a dream and wondered who you were?

Hyland sat bolt upright in a near state of panic. He found himself reaching for support as if the bus he had dreamed he was on was making a sharp turn. As his mind started to clear, Hyland suddenly realized that it had all been a dream. The belt, the amazing suit, Johnny Rapid... Wait! Who is Johnny Rapid??

Falling back onto his pillow, Hyland remembered his trip to school just the day before. It had been raining and brought gloom to the start of his day. This was a familiar feeling. Yesterday, when the bus arrived, he was already in a foul mood.

"Good morning!" said the cheery bus driver.

Julie, their loyal bus driver, had seemingly been behind the yellow transport's wheel since the Confederacy lost to the Union armies. She was in her mid-sixties and in excellent health. Julie's career as a school-student delivery service was now approaching forty-three years of duty.

Hylan always took the seat right behind Julie's. He knew that he could always get a warm welcome. Unfortunately, his hopes for a pleasant distraction from the rain were shattered when two local bullies decided to target Hylan with their verbal assaults.

His only defense to bullies was to either take the abuse or run away. Sadly, sitting on a moving bus tends to make retreat impossible. Hylan sat in the front of the bus for Julie's support and to make a quick exit as soon as they reached school.

It was rare that any of the confrontations Hylan had endured led to something physical. But, just the lack of support from his peers made even the verbal jibes painful.

Sitting up in his bed, Hyland's mind returned to the present. He started to think about his dream. Who was Johnny Rapid? How did Johnny Rapid take down the bullies? Did the belt give him superpowers? If so, is it possible to make these *powers* a reality?

A quiet knock on his door by his mom alerted Hylan that another day of torment was about to begin. He slowly dragged himself out of bed, got dressed, and went through the motions necessary to arrive at school successfully.

Hylan was not much of a daydreamer. However, today, he found himself contemplating just who Johnny Rapid was. His day's events were a dull blur. All Hylan wanted to do was get home, climb back into bed, and get back to that magical belt.

CHAPTER 4.
THE REVELATION

———•··◆··•———

Time could not pass fast enough for Hylan. His fifth-grade year of school had taught him two things. First, even though he was more intelligent than everyone else in his class, his good grades made him even more of an outsider. Secondly, he wished he could sleep 17 hours a day and be awake only to eat and play Pokémon.

But in a way, Hylan was gaining wisdom from his dreams. He encountered his belt and his superhero identity almost every single night. His days passed by with minimal incidents, his time spent concentrating on his school work. While his nights allowed him to recharge his proverbial batteries as he took retribution against the bullies. He learned that Johnny Rapid made it possible to build up his own ego and inner strength by assisting others with their plights. In fact, his superhero persona made it possible for just his presence as Johnny Rapid to intimidate anyone wanting to hurt another.

Hylan's birthday was in late August. One of the reasons he was tormented was because he was always the youngest person in his class. Plus, he was small in stature for his age and soft-spoken. The combination made him an easy target for the bullies.

During the summer before six-grade, Hylan came to an important revelation. It didn't matter how big or small he was. His *smarts* were almost irrelevant. What mattered in a world full of one-upmanship was to be able to fall back on one's skills. And, when that failed, to be able to rely on one's brawn to win the day. So, that lonely summer, Hylan started to become more active. Instead of sitting around all day, he went out to play. He began to imagine what a superhero would do to get into shape and maintain it.

Going back to school that fall was a new starting point for everyone in his class. Entering the six-grade meant that three local elementary schools would be combining their students into the middle school. Six grade opened up many opportunities that were not available to him before.

Hylan did not know what to expect when he arrived at the larger school. He had spent the summer primarily alone and was a bit overwhelmed by the new environment. Hylan had promised himself that he would not allow bullying. However, his new attitude brought him a different kind of trouble.

He wanted his superhero persona to take over. But, Hylan did so by acting out and becoming the center of attention. By choosing to use his innate intelligence not to stand out as a student but to react to almost everything sarcastically, he became an annoying distraction to his teachers. His desire to become popular among his peers made the school's staff just plain mad.

It didn't take long for Hylan to end up in detention and spending time after school with the miscreants. Getting himself into trouble became just a part of his life.

Then, it happened. Walking into detention that day, Hylan was confronted by Mr. O'Grady. Hylan didn't get three feet into the classroom when O'Grady took him by the shoulder and directed him to a seat in the front row.

"I want you up-front here where I can keep an eye on you," said O'Grady with an Irish brogue that made Hylan cringe. O'Grady stood at six-foot-two and weighed in at a solid 220 lbs. The man's demeanor and attitude screamed athlete and a person not to antagonize. There were only four other students in detention that day. Hylan started to worry that something odd was going on.

In the past, school detention sessions were made up of kids who, for whatever reason, were either misbehaving or not following the rules while in class. The group in front of Mr. O'Grady was made up of repeat offenders.

O'Grady started to speak, "Okay, y'all. You're here because I asked for you. Let me tell you a story…"

Hylan found himself sighing and starting to worry. How much trouble was he in this time?

"I used to be a self-obsessed bully when I was in school," said O'Grady. "I was bigger than the other kids in my class. So, like a lunkhead, I thought I could be the *big man on campus* by picking on the loners and outsiders. I was about your age when I decided to try out for football. I quickly got my head handed to me time and time again until I learned how to be more of a team player. My coach said something to me that made me really think. He told me that life is not about just you! You're going to be a lonely son-of-a-bitch if you don't start learning about your fellow classmates rather than picking on them. He then sat me down and forced me to tell him what I knew about the other football team members. It turned out I knew nothing."

As O'Grady kept talking, Hylan started to think about this. What did he know about anyone else in school? Maybe, he should try to find a club or a team to join. For the first time in his life, Hylan decided to *join* something rather than ridicule and avoid the people who did.

It turned out that the man standing in front of him was not just *Mister* O-Grady. He was *Coach* O'Grady of the wrestling team. It was right then that Hylan decided to try out.

After detention ended and looking like a dog who had just been caught misbehaving with its tail between its legs, Hylan waited until the classroom had cleared. Now, alone with Coach O'Grady, Hylan asked, "Can I join the wrestling team?"

O'Grady inwardly smiled and said, "You mean *try out* for the wrestling team. We only take the best, you know. What makes you think you can live up to my standards?"

Hylan decided to stand his ground. He felt his superhero alter ego coming alive and said, "What makes you think I can't? I can do anything I put my mind to."

Impressed with what he saw in the diminutive lad, O'Grady retorted, "Everybody gets a chance in my book. You be in the gym after seventh period tomorrow. We'll do some training, and then I'll give you a shot." O'Grady was an excellent evaluator of his students. He saw something in Hylan. He wasn't quite sure what. But, he believed that there was something deep inside this kid that could blossom into an athlete.

Hylan stepped back and said, "I'll be there. And, I'll show you that I can do anything." With that said and not looking back, Hylan walked out of the classroom.

"Could this be it?" muttered Hylan to himself. Without realizing it, Hylan was standing tall. His typically slouched appearance faded, and the confidence he felt when he was wearing his magic belt seemed to take over. "I'll show him," Hylan thought to himself. "I'll be the greatest wrestler in this school's history."

He didn't notice it at the time. Hylan exuded the confidence that only appeared when he wore his magic belt. Because he had been in detention and missed the bus, he had to wait for his Mom to pick him up after she got off work. Yet, Hylan did not feel lonely. He did not feel insecure.

Would the decision to take up Coach O'Grady's challenge make a difference in his life? Only time would tell.

CHAPTER 5.
TURNING POINTS

———•··•◆•··•———

The magic belt was going to remain a secret. For that matter, so was Johnny Rapid. Hylan's bedtime was no longer the focus of his life. As a wrestler, it turned out that Hylan was the best in his weight class. Although he looked forward to his dreams, they were no longer the center of his life.

Sixth grade and his new interest in a sport he could dominate hardened Hylan's belief that he was a superhero. Although he was still tormented by a few boys from his old elementary school, the incidents were far and in between.

In the sport of wrestling, the weight classes allow anyone who can pass the appropriate physical to participate and legitimately compete. For the first time in Hylan's life, his small stature could be turned into an asset. He wrestled in the lowest weight class. Eventually, his abilities grew to the point where he could perform well against larger opponents. The difference between an average wrestler and a great one was strategy and technique. Hylan maximized both skills and took to heart the excellent lessons taught by Coach O'Grady.

However, something had changed in Hylan. His growing confidence amplified his desire to be idolized. Adulation came with his success as a wrestler. But of greater importance was his belief that the magic belt in his dreams was somehow with him when he was awake. For a while, Hylan worried that he was still dreaming. But it wasn't long before he figured out how to tell when he was asleep or awake. All he had to do was look down. If he was wearing the magic belt, he was asleep.

Sixth grade led to seventh and seventh grade led to eighth. Almost with every growing day, Hylan became more self-assured. His confidence must have shown because he found himself surrounded by female classmates all of the time. Hylan was a good-looking guy with a friendly personality. He stood out as a real catch when you threw in his success on the mat.

Middle school is usually a challenge for adolescents, especially boys, at least from their point of view. Interestingly enough, Hylan almost sailed through the traumas of middle school. His popularity among the young ladies continued to grow. He found himself hanging out with older girls, which only increased his confidence in himself.

The only nagging annoyance was one bully from his old elementary school days. Like most bullies, Sean Thornton had his own issues. He was overweight and just slightly more intelligent than a tree stump. When you added in his abusive home environment, it wasn't surprising that he acted out. Sean was Hylan's only remaining tormenter. Jealousy also was a factor. Seeing Hylan with an entourage of young ladies could not have helped raise Sean's self-esteem. Hylan could be having a great day. But as soon as he was alone, it wasn't unusual for Sean to throw out insults, do things like purple nurples, try to trip him, knock his books out of his arm, or just be a total prick.

On the other hand, it was a large school, and Sean did not hang out with any of Hylan's newfound friends. For Hylan, it was frustrating.

Fortunately, the incidents no longer came to blows. So, Hylan, for the most part, just blew them off.

In some ways, middle school was a significant turning point for Hylan. He wasn't just becoming the superhero from his dreams. Hylan realized that as long as he performed well as a wrestler, he could maintain the level of adoration he craved. He still enjoyed his dreams and the powers his magic belt bestowed upon him. But, now, he could realize his potential to become a real-life hero to his classmates.

Things only seemed to get better when he entered high school.

Hylan's self-assurance dramatically increased as he grew into manhood. His wrestling and daily workouts kept him at the top of his game. His success on the mat helped him maintain his popularity. He found himself dating the girls of his choice rather than being forced to fantasize about them from a distance like so many of his peers.

His gain in self-confidence was also reflected in his grades. Although quite bright, in the past, he tended to blow off school work. Now, he was one of the top students in his class.

And date, he did. Unless Hylan was under the weather, he was out every weekend with his pals and always had a date on Saturday night. Because of his popularity, it was a rarity that his dates were not juniors or seniors in school. To make matters even better, it was those older young ladies that sought him out.

The climax of his tenth-grade year came literally on the field of play.

The so-called in-crowd was divided between the wrestling team hanging out with the soccer players and the football players staying pretty much to themselves. This social schism caused competition for the fairer sex and a continuing war of words. Even though soccer was very popular, the varsity cheerleaders performed for the football players. The junior varsity cheerleaders who strived to become varsity were relegated to the soccer team. It may seem petty, but this out-of-date tradition reached a boiling point that climaxed on the school's athletic field.

It wasn't that the wrestling team favored the soccer players. Circumstances and friendships by happenstance had just developed that way. When a verbal fight broke out between the captain of the football team and the soccer team's head goalie, all hell resulted.

The two seniors were interested in the same girl. Abby Pordeca was a very well-put-together young lady on the varsity cheerleading squad. She was just a junior but had qualified to move from junior varsity to varsity. Typically, only seniors were on the varsity squad. As silly as it sounds, the football players felt that the varsity squad of cheerleaders belonged to them. To complicate things, the school's soccer goalie had been dating Abby. But when she joined the more prestigious varsity squad, the school's star quarterback thought that he had the first choice before anyone else in school. It didn't seem to matter to him what the target of his amorous affections thought about this.

The verbal fight between the two athletes led to angry words and a challenge to fight. Both young men knew they would spend most of the next two weeks in detention if they laid a hand on the other inside the high school. So, off they went to the adjacent baseball field just out of sight of the main campus.

Of course, their argument had not gone unheard. Sides were already being drawn up, and the grapevine mill spread the news of the fight faster than a cheetah on the hunt.

The two combatants wouldn't follow the Marquess of Queensbury Rules and have a classic boxing match. This would be an all-out street fight, with both of them hoping to put the other in the hospital. Sadly, the possibility of a brutal battle made the growing audience full of glee. By the time the quarterback and goalie were about to face off, betting was already taking place among the crowd.

The first punch was yet to land when derisive remarks came from other football team members aimed at the soccer players. Almost immediately, Hylan found himself taking sides.

Hylan's innate confidence had grown to the point that he thought he was always in the right. When two of his friends on the soccer team were confronted by four football squad members, he stepped in. The first punch ended up not being thrown by either the quarterback or the goalie. The brawl started when a 190-pound linebacker took a swing at Hyland… and missed.

One punch, then two slammed into faces. Because of Hylan's involvement and the existing friendships, the wrestling team joined the soccer players in choosing the nearest football player to confront. The sides were more or less evenly matched in numbers. On the other hand, it turned out that the wrestling team had quite an advantage. For the most part, the soccer and football players may have been good at team sports. But, they were not trained in a one-on-one competition like the wrestlers were. What literally was an all-out war knockdown drag-out fight ended only when the three coaches arrived on the scene and broke up the melee.

Blood and bruises were everywhere. But it was decisive. With the assistance of the soccer players, the wrestling team had laid waste to the football players. And ironically, the quarterback and goalie who had started the entire mess were unscathed. They just watched as their teammates wreaked havoc.

Hylan and his compatriots were not the worse for wear for the most part. Wrestlers are trained to maintain control of their situation. With everything that had commenced, Hylan had thrown not a single punch. Although he had taken down no fewer than four opponents in less than two minutes, he had done it using skill, leverage, and the understanding of just where the vulnerable, weak points were located on the human body.

The thrill from their success over the football players was short-lived. The expected finger-pointing and accusations started to fly. The result was a record-setting detention class that took place on the football field for five days. None of the participants were left out. The three coaches forced all of the players to attend and to ensure that everyone involved was accounted for. Believe me. After three hours of running stadiums, the players had learned their lesson.

But after all of this, who got the girl?

Well, a wrestler had won! Soon after the fight and the week-long bout with a detention class that would have made an Army special forces member blush, Hylan started to date Abby!

The most popular girl in school would not only steal Hylan's heart, but she would become possibly the most crucial turning point in our superhero's life.

PART II.
GROWING UP TOO FAST

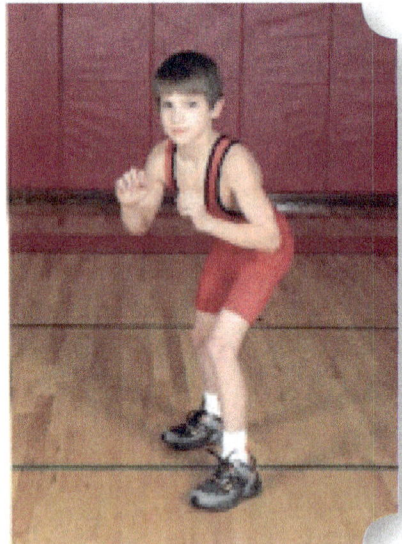

CHAPTER 6.
CHOICES

——————•·••·—◆—·••·•——————

High school is like being in a time warp. How you got there is almost completely forgotten in favor of the irrational assumption that the good, bad, and the ugly will never end.

For Hylan Taylor, the good by far outweighed the bad and the ugly. He was number one in his weight class as a wrestler, the center of his growing group of friends, and dated the most popular girl in school.

Abby turned out to be a great blessing for Hylan. He did not share his nighttime dreams with her. In his mind, Abby had become his real-life magical belt. His relationship with her had become as strong as the bond he had with his imaginary belt. In some ways, Abby made him feel even more like a superhero. She treated him well and covered for any social missteps Hylan may have made. Abby was Hylan's end-all. For maybe the first time in his life, Hylan felt complete. He still enjoyed his nighttime dreams regularly. But, he found himself checking to see if he was wearing his magical belt less and less often.

Hylan was living the high life of a senior in high school. And he was only a sophomore. His diminutive stature was no longer an obstacle. His wrestling abilities proved that size only mattered to those less intelligent than himself. He believed his smarts were responsible for nearly everything he enjoyed. His first year in high school seemed to be a window to just how great the rest of his life would be.

But things changed, and the unexpected happened.

Abby and Hylan were the toast of the town in their high school class. They had a wonderful time together over the summer and continued their romance into the new school year. Abby was about a year and a half older than Hylan. When she became a senior, Hylan was just entering the 11th grade. Life was going well through the Christmas holidays, including a New Year's Eve get-together party that would have made a rowdy bachelor's party seem timid.

The two lovers lived on opposite sides of town. Yet, they always were able to figure out ways to get together. Even in school, they found themselves hand-in-hand almost everywhere but in class.

In late January of Hylan's junior year, they were enjoying an unusually warm day with a walk through the center of town. When they came to a small public park, Abby told Hylan that she wanted to sit down.

Abby became fidgety and started to look around. She was still holding Hylan's hand but bouncing it up and down on her knee. He was becoming uncomfortable as he waited for her to say something. It was as if he was sitting next to a ticking time bomb waiting to go off. He said, "Are you okay?"

Then Hylan was hit with the news. Abby was pregnant!

"What are we going to do?" asked Abby.

Thinking for a couple of seconds, Hylan found himself inwardly excited. He said, "Well, do you want to keep the baby?"

Abby was annoyed at the response. It had never occurred to her to abort her child. Her emotional state was like a rollercoaster ride gone crazy. She said, "I would never give up my baby. The only question I have for you is, *are you with me or against me?*"

Hylan had no time to think about what to do. He was running on instincts. His mind was telling him to run away together. His gut was saying *stay*. He said, "Hey, we're in this together. This is my baby, too. Whatever you think you need me to do is fine. We'll figure this out!"

Abby wasn't sure if she was relieved or dismayed. Did she really love Hylan? The answer to herself was, "Yes." Did she want to spend the rest of her life with him? Was he going to be a good father, and would he be able to support her? She didn't know. After all, Hylan was only good in two areas, in bed and on the mat.

Still holding Abby's hand, Hylan asked, "So, what's our next move? Are you sure about your condition?"

"My condition?" said an antsy Abby. "It's not like I have the plague or something. I'm pregnant. I went through three tests. We were careless. We were… We were…" Abby started to cry.

Not knowing what else to do, Hylan let Abby melt into his arms and hugged her. She placed her head on his shoulder and continued to weep. The two of them sat on the bench for what seemed like an eternity.

"Okay, okay," said Hylan. Thinking quickly, he continued, "Why don't we tell our parents that we are staying at friends' houses, and we go to our hangout instead? That way, we can think things out and plan what to do."

Hylan didn't have a lot of money. He did some side jobs but nothing steady. On the other hand, Abby's stepdad had his own business. Although he was not wealthy, he did give Abby a reasonable allowance. Although Hylan paid for their dates and any expenses that came with going steady, Abby paid for the more expensive things like their occasional motel room.

Off they went together to their *hangout*, better known as the Starlight Motel. It was their regular haunt and probably where they conceived their soon-to-be offspring. They also used the place as an escape for Abby when her stepfather became abusive.

The Starlight Motel may have sounded romantic, and it could be. The old motel was located off Interstate 85 in Gwinnett County, Georgia, near where they lived. It was made up of two buildings; one fronting the street and one out of sight behind the main facility. The street-side building was favored by overnight travelers. But the second building had developed the local reputation as a place to go to have a *good time*.

As you might have guessed, there was a lot of cash used when registering for a room in the *back building*, as it was called. Although technically illegal, the owners understood that many guests did not want a record of their say. Or, for that matter, how many hours they stayed. The management had *special* amenities to cater to their clientele, like custom lighting, jacuzzies, and mirrored ceilings. It was one of these rooms that Abby loved and always picked for their nocturnal mischief.

Arriving at room B205, Hylan slipped the keycard into the door and popped the lock. They were not there to have a good time as much as wanting a private place to talk. He closed the door, turned on the lights, and pulled two cushioned chairs face-to-face by the bed. Sitting across from each other, Hylan spoke up, "Are you going to be okay?"

"Of course I am," said Abby. "It's not like I'm the first person ever to get pregnant!" Every time she said the word *pregnant*, she winced. She knew that her life was over as she had known it. Her challenge was getting Hylan to understand that, too.

They talked for the better part of an hour. Having already lied to their parents about where they were staying that night, Hylan and Abby decided to try and get a good night's sleep. It was Friday night. So, they had the weekend to plan before school on Monday.

Hylan and Abby were in love. Or, at least, as in love as two teenagers could be. They chose to stay together and do their best to take care of each other. With this in mind and realizing they had no place to go in the morning, they decided to do what they did best.

Hylan took Abby into his arms, kissed her, and caressed her shapely figure. It didn't take long for their clothes to end up on the floor and the bed to become a tangled mess. They shared a giggle about not needing to worry about birth control and went at it like two lovers separated by war and reunited for the first time in months.

It was as if a huge weight had been lifted off Abby's shoulders. She no longer worried that Hylan would abandon her. Somehow, everything would work out.

On the other hand, Hylan wasn't sure about anything except his love for Abby. What were they going to do? He hoped that they could figure that out fast. In the meantime, he was making love to the most popular girl in school, and she was all his.

But, for now, they were physically one. Had they also become of one mind, too. Abby and Hylan thought so, but for different reasons.

Their decision was made. On Sunday, they would go home and pack whatever they could carry. Abby would tell her parents that she would *borrow* a car, and the two lovebirds would run away together to places unknown.

CHAPTER 7.

ON THE ROAD

Places-unknown. How could a place be unknown? Well, that's what Abby and Hylan were about to find out.

They thought about traveling to California. But, between the two of them, they had less than $500. So, wherever they went, it had to be far enough away not to be found but relatively easy to access. So, like so many people, they headed for Florida. Hylan's thought about this was, "At least it would be warm."

Their decision to run away was mainly chosen out of fear. Hylan knew that his mother would be supportive. It was Abby's stepdad that terrified them both. Abby and Hylan knew that her father would force Abby to have an abortion. She also believed that if she told her mom, daddy would immediately find out.

Homer, Abby's stepdad, was not the best of people. He was known locally as redneck white trash. He swore all the time, had a short fuse, used intimidation to get what he wanted, and could melt steel by breathing on it with his rotten breath. And that's how Abby described him.

Hylan's relationship with him wasn't much better. Although the couple never disclosed the intimate component of their relationship to Homer, he was very sure that his daughter was not exactly still a virgin. The only saving grace that allowed Homer to tolerate Hylan dating his daughter was their reputation for being the school's king and queen. Homer actually got off on his daughter being so popular. Considering that without exception, anyone who knew Homer thought he was slime, he could shamelessly live vicariously knowing that Abby was so desired.

Hylan's mom vacationed in a small community on the Florida panhandle called Panama City. He knew that the beachfront properties and hotels were expensive. However, there were a bunch of affordable long-term-stay motels available in town. He also believed they could easily find work since most kids their age would be in school.

Something they did argue about was school. Hylan was a good student and knew he would miss wrestling and graduation. Abby's attitude was that she couldn't care less. At best, she was an A+ student but had little use for school or a diploma. Neither of her parents had graduated from school. Her father had a successful small business. Abby's mom was able to be a stay-at-home wife because of it. Abby had her mom's looks and her dad's tenacity. So, she believed between Hylan and herself that they would be fine.

Upon arriving in Panama City, they quickly found a motel. The place was not exactly the Ritz. But, it was clean and cheap. The latter being most important. After checking in and being relieved that they could pay with cash, they ventured up to their room.

Abby flipped on the light switch and said, "Hmmm, home sweet home."

Hylan responded, "For now. This place is fine until we can get a permanent home." He then kicked off his sneakers and jumped on the king-sized bed.

Watching him bounce up and down on the bed, Abby said, "Would you like some company?" She had already started to undress. When Hylan looked over and tried to agree, Abby was already down to her bright pink panties. Placing one knee on the bed, Abby bounced once and then landed squarely on top of Hylan.

He started to caress Abby and quickly realized that her panties were still on. He said, "Don't you think you should take these things off?"

Abby straddled Hylan's thighs and said, "This from the guy who still has all his clothes on?" Then, mimicking Scarlett O'Hara, she retorted, "*I'm feeling so faint and may pass out if you don't find some way to rescue me. Oh, whatever shall I do?*"

The two lovebirds again did what they do best. The rest of the day was spent in bed, trying to forget about the rest of the world. But that was only a temporary respite. They both knew that tomorrow's *another day* would bring them far more challenges than poor Scarlett O'Hara would ever have to endure.

The following day, Abby and Hylan decided to take the week off and check out the beach. They would wait until the following Monday to find work. After all, they were sure that there would be plenty of jobs.

To their dismay, adulting proved to be a greater challenge than they expected.

The later 2000s saw one of the most significant economic crashes in the history of the United States. Hylan and Abby chose one of the worst times to look for work. Most, if not all, businesses were struggling with downsizing decisions that rarely included hiring a pair of teenagers. Although Abby and Hylan could find some part-time work, neither could find a full-time job, much less work that paid any benefits.

It didn't take long for their finances to run out. Their desire to be on their own ended up being overtaken by a need to maintain a roof over their head. Just over three weeks had gone by since their abrupt departure from Georgia. Now the pressure was on. What should they do next?

By this time, Abby and Hylan's parents knew about the pregnancy. The young couple had lied about their whereabouts and the fact that they were not working. Hylan's mom was distressed. And interestingly enough, Abby's parents were showing the same kind of concern.

Abby's mom was a sweetheart. She went out of her way to make Homer, her husband, as happy as possible. Unfortunately, she was submissive and without an opinion of her own. If Homer said that it was one way, then Abby's mom was fully supportive.

What surprised Abby was her mom saying they were welcome to come back and stay with them. To Abby, this meant that her stepdad had agreed to let them come home. She was also astonished by the offer to give Hylan a job if they did return.

Abby and Hylan decided to move back north with their money running out and their options almost nonexistent. Abby's parents lived in southern Tennessee near the Georgia border. So, off they went.

It had been a month since they had run away. They learned from their adventure that it would be difficult for them to live on their own. Hylan and Abby decided that the best plan would be to live with her parents and find work.

After all, they loved each other and could tolerate anything for a short time. Right? Well, this was their plan. They would move in with Abby's parents, find work, have their baby, and live happily ever after. Just like Scarlett O'Hara. The world was theirs for the taking. All they had to do was reach out and grab it. Yeah, nothing could go wrong there.

CHAPTER 8.

GROWING UP TOO QUICKLY

Working for Homer wasn't as bad as Hylan thought it would be. Abby had pushed him to take the job, which basically entailed doing whatever Homer told him to do. It wasn't hard work. But, Hylan knew it was a dead-end position that allowed Homer to spend more time hunting than working.

Abby's parents made her go back to high school. She objected because of her pregnancy. But, her mom told her that she would be done and graduate before she started to show. Hylan decided to take a different route. He chose to continue his full-time job and complete high school through an online program. Because he was a good student, Hylan had already completed the required classes to graduate. He wasn't sure why having the diploma was so important. College was never really a consideration. But at least he could say that he completed something and, maybe, it would be important for obtaining a better job.

That summer, Abby gave birth to their daughter. They named her Kylie. Abby's mom proved to be a huge blessing to Abby. The young mother loved her daughter but was almost clueless about taking care of her. Abby and her mom bonded over their love for Kylie. This eventually evolved into the doting grandmother caring for Kylie while her daughter looked for work.

Abby chose the restaurant industry for her first job. She knew that wait staff made the bulk of their money from tips. So, she looked at places where tips might be more abundant. You can imagine how thrilled Hylan was when he came home to find Abby in the uniform of a Hooter's wait staff member. Abby was all excited about how great the tips would be. Hylan just stood there and worried about how attractive she looked in the outfit.

Hylan had difficulty transitioning from a popular high schooler and successful athlete to becoming a go-for to his girlfriend's dad. Most of his day was spent doing repetitive tasks that any kid could do... Oh yeah, he was one of those kids! In frustration, he found himself struggling with pent-up anger. He tried to release it by throwing rocks at whatever inanimate object he could find after work. His one solace was his newborn daughter. When he was with her, all his inner strife faded away.

One tedious day led to the next for Hylan. The only change came from Abby. She was coming home later and later almost every night. Supposedly, she worked seven days a week to bring in extra money. But Hylan was getting concerned.

When Abby started her job at Hooters, very little changed in their relationship. She would come home in that sexy uniform and regularly entertain Hylan with passionate kisses that led to a striptease that quickly found the couple entangled in whatever place they found convenient to do what they did best together.

Several months passed by with almost imperceptible changes happening with Abby's demeanor toward both Hylan and Kylie. Her hours became longer and longer, her arrival home later and later. Claiming to be tired and worn out from work, their sex life quickly went from a four-alarm fire to almost nonexistent.

Hylan was a doting father. When he was not working, he spent as much time as possible with his daughter. But, the time Abby spent with Kylie ended up being covered more frequently by her mom.

It wasn't until an unusually personal conversation with Homer that Hylan started to get suspicious.

Typically, Homer was gruff and, many times, obnoxious with Hylan. Then one day after work, he took Hylan aside and asked, "Hey man, you're a better man than me. I could never put up with my gal flirting and wearing those clothes that Abby has to wear for work. How do you do it?"

The first thing that ran through Hylan's mind was not about Abby but about Homer. This was the first time that he came across as almost human. Hylan was used to keeping his guard up when dealing with him. Then, Hylan started to think about what Homer meant.

Hylan said, "It's okay. I know she loves me. She's just doing what she needs to do to get extra tips."

Homer retorted, "Well, if it was me. I'd be more worried." With that said, Homer turned and went to do whatever he did in the bathroom that usually made it smell like a hazardous waste dump.

Believing that he was not concerned and that Homer was overthinking things, Hylan went into his daughter's room. While she was happily sleeping, he started to think about what Abby was doing. After a few minutes, he found himself becoming concerned.

Hylan's concerns were deserved. He didn't know that Abby was *not* working during many of those extra hours. He realized that there may have been more to his picking up and dropping Abby off at work and other places around town. Was there something to worry about?

Abby had supposedly made many *friends* at Hooters. To help her out, Hylan regularly dropped her off at some of these friends' houses. He had blown off her use of the work *dates* when it came to many of the visits. Because he worked during the day, it hadn't occurred to him that many of these so-called *dates* were all at night, sometimes very late at night. Was there something going on?

For the first time since knowing Abby, Hylan found himself getting jealous.

Having little to do on the weekends, Hylan started dropping into the Hooters, where Abby worked. Numerous times, he caught her flirting with customers. It was not unusual for certain guests to get extra *favors* by tipping more. Abby told Hylan that she was only acting her role as eye candy for the flirty few. She had little, if any, interest in the clientele she served. She played her part to the hilt and compensated well for her troubles.

Yet, now, Hylan wondered if there was more going on. Little Miss Innocent was just doing her job… right? But what was she doing after work? What was going on during those late-night get-togethers she had several nights during the week and on the weekend?

Abby had always been overly sensitive about her looks. This was sad because she looked gorgeous even first thing in the morning when just getting out of bed. Abby tended to wear too much makeup and felt it necessary to spend way too much time reorganizing her hair. However, it made her happy. So, Hylan tended to blow it off.

What started to concern Hylan was that her skin tone and hairdo seemed to change every week. It was one thing to primp one's hair and put on makeup daily. But the changes to her hair and her constant tan seemed to be a bit overboard, even for a Hooters' girl.

Hylan's jealousy and frustration with Abby's supposedly busy work schedule led him to spy on her. He started to follow Abby to work. To his surprise, Abby regularly stopped at the tanning and hair salon just down the street. Sometimes, she was there for just a few minutes. But other times, she didn't come out for quite some time.

One night after Abby had fallen asleep, Hylan quietly got up from bed and went over to her night table. Unplugging her cellphone from its charger, he tiptoed out of the room and into the empty living room space. He then entered Abby's password into her phone and started to scroll.

He began with her texts and traced the names he didn't know to their contact pages. It didn't take long to discover that the owner of the local tanning salon and Abby were having intimate conversations.

When Abby woke up and found Hylan with her phone, she again became defensive and was angered by Hylan intruding on what she told him was her private space. She took the phone away from Hylan and said, "That's my phone! You know, I don't mind you playing games on it, but you have no right to go through my messages! I have to play games with my clientele. You just don't understand!

Not wanting to make things any worse, Hylan handed her phone back to her. She turned it off and shoved it into her purse.

Later that week, Abby inadvertently forgot to take her phone with her to work. Hylan was surprised at this. She had spent a small fortune to purchase the top-of-the-line Sidekick phone. The somewhat cumbersome unit had one of the first full keyboards available at a time when most were still flip phones. He wondered how someone could forget something like that. Then, he found himself once again scrolling through her texts.

What he found were more intimate conversations that obviously were in response to multiple affairs. He discovered his anger building up inside, like a volcano, just before an eruption. He wasn't jealous as much as mad. He loved Abby so much and believed that they could work through anything. She didn't have to lie to him. Yet, that's what he confirmed in his own mind. She was lying all the time!

Looking at her most recent text, Hylan went to her contact page and found the sender's number. He called the number using Abby's phone. When the party on the other end answered with an intimate nickname, Hylan spoke up, asking if he was dating Abby.

Obviously surprised that it wasn't Abby on the line, the guy immediately denied even knowing Abby. But Hylan wasn't fooled. Why would his number be on her contact page and day after day of texting be from someone who didn't know who she was?

Mad as hell, Hylan left the house, climbed into his car, and drove directly to Hooters. He stormed in, demanding to know where Abby was. When Abby saw Hylan in an almost hysterical state, she quickly packed up her things, took him by the arm, and left work to avoid making things worse.

After they got into Hylan's car, he asked about the salon owner. Not knowing that he knew about their affair, she lied. Hylan confronted her while driving home with the information he had discovered on her phone the night before. Abby got so angry that she hit Hylan with a 32-ounce cup of soda.

Already angry with his adrenaline pumping out of control. Hylan reacted without thinking. He smacked Abby in the face and inadvertently broke her tooth.

Hylan was horrified by his own actions. His anger and jealousy instantly disappeared, replaced by intense regret and overwhelming shock caused by his actions.

Their short-lived fight immediately stopped resulting in total silence as Hylan pulled into Homer's driveway. Abby got out of the car, slammed the door, then stormed into the house crying. Before Hylan could get up the front steps, he was confronted by an enraged Homer.

As soon as Abby had entered the house, she went straight to her dad. Homer immediately noticed the chipped tooth and asked her what had happened. After guiding his daughter to the sofa and sitting her down, Homer practically ran Hylan over as he strode out the front door.

Homer then contemplated an opportunity. He put up with Hylan when the two kids were in high school together. It annoyed him that Hylan was so brilliant compared to himself. Homer knew that he could do little, if anything, about Abby and Hylan's relationship. He was well aware of the Romeo and Juliet syndrome. Trying to come between what he considered two star-crossed lovers would only drive them closer together. So, he put up with it. When Abby got pregnant, he knew that by forcing the issue, they would stay runaways. By letting them come home, he had some control over their lives.

But this was too much.

This 17-year-old kid had hit his daughter. This was not to be tolerated whatsoever in any way. Rather than starting a fight with the ex-wrestler, Homer decided to call the police.

The community they lived in was not exactly a roaring metropolis. Each week, the number of incidents involving police, other than traffic violations, could be counted on one hand. When the assault complaint came in, both deputies on duty jumped into a patrol car and sped off to address Homer's complaint.

The complaint led to a he-said-she-said argument that just frustrated the officers. A formal incident report was written and basically said that Hylan did a no-no. One of the officers knew Abby well from Hooters. He wished they could write that *she got what was coming,* and *Homer beating the tar out of Hylan would have been justified.* The result was a lot of hurt feelings and Hylan being told that he had to find another place to live, at least for now.

Hylan packed up his things, said goodbye to his daughter, climbed into his old Acura Integra, and drove off to Georgia. His destination was home. Or, at least, the only home he had known before choosing to run away in the first place. He had already called ahead, and his mom expected him before midnight.

The ride home proved to Hylan that he needed to be prepared for anything. About halfway into his trip, the timing belt snapped. To make matters even worse, his cell phone was dead. After walking over three miles to the nearest gas station, he finally got ahold of his mom. Arriving home with his car literally in tow, Hylan started to wonder if the day's events were some kind of an omen.

Hylan would be turning 18 soon. His birthday was just a few days away. In most cultures, the all-important age of 18 meant adulthood. For Hylan, he had grown up too quickly. He had gone from childhood to adulthood responsibilities in less than six months. Now, he had to decide just what to do.

CHAPTER 9.
THE BIG STEP

—◆—

Hylan's mom greeted him with open arms. They rarely had the opportunity to see each other after Hylan's untimely departure to Florida with Abby.

His mom quickly became Hylan's greatest supporter. Her career had always been the center of her life. With the return of her son, she dedicated as much time as possible to Hylan's needs. In many ways, it was as if the stress brought on by years of sometimes overwhelming challenges had nearly disappeared for the both of them.

Things were different since Hylan had last been home. His bedroom, his sanctuary, had been completely changed. After Abby and Hylan chose to move in with Abby's parents, Hylan's mom decided to update everything in his room except the bed. The walls were painted a different color, and the threadbare rug had been replaced. Even the light fixtures and furniture had been changed.

But the room was still his. Within seconds of entering it and placing his stuff on the bed, he suddenly realized that he hadn't been dreaming at night… at all. Happy memories of his magical belt and all the amazing things he could do flooded his mind.

When he returned to the living room, Simon was sitting there with Hylan's mom.

Shortly after moving to their new home after the fire and living in a camper, Hylan's mom met Simon. They had dated only a short time before his mom readily accepted his offer of marriage.

Hylan's mom was a loving and caring person but had a dominating personality. Everything had to be the way she wanted it but in a *nice* way. Her job was as a purchasing manager for a large consumer product distribution company. She was perfect for the job with her eye for detail.

Her strict ways had kept Hylan more or less on the straight and narrow. It wasn't until Abby got pregnant that he defied her by going off on his own. She was also saddened by Hylan and Abby choosing to move to Tennessee to stay with Homer.

Simon was a sweetheart who saw the joy in most everything. He found Hylan's mom to be a tempest in a teacup that needed to be savored and enjoyed. He brought tenderness and love to the home and was a perfect fit for Hylan's mom. Hylan had grown to respect the man as a father.

Simon laid down some simple rules. First, Hylan needed to find a job. He needed to have something to do every day. Second, they did not want him to mope around. Any help Hylan felt he required would be immediately addressed. In many ways, his return home allowed Hylan to get his head on straight and move ahead.

That night, Hylan's dreams returned. He found himself back in superhero mode and raring to make the world a better place. The morning brought a fresh start for Hylan. He decided that his first goal would be to find a job.

Valueline Instant Oil Change had a large sign out in front of their local dealership that said, *Help Wanted, No experience necessary*. In Hylan's mind, this meant he was highly qualified for the position.

Hylan stepped into the waiting area and spoke to the first employee he saw. He was immediately escorted to the manager's office for a brief interview. After about ten minutes of questions and answers, the manager, named Greg, gave Hylan a packet of paperwork to review and fill out.

Hylan went back to the waiting room and opened the envelope. The application was only two pages. It was the aptitude test that took up all of the room. Many corporations require a general knowledge and aptitude test as part of their hiring package. Theoretically, it was so a prospect could be placed in the best position possible. In reality, it was because the powers that be in the business were just plain nosy.

It didn't take long for Hylan to blow through the paperwork. He slid the documents back into the envelope and returned to Greg's office. Hylan was surprised that Greg only reviewed the application. He left the test in the envelope and dropped it into a basket marked *Outgoing-Corporate*. With no explanation forthcoming, Greg continued the interview. He said, "Everything looks good! If you're up for it, you can start tomorrow as the supply clerk to the mechanics."

Hylan knew from working with Homer that this meant he would be back to being a go-for. But the job paid well, and the hours were good. He agreed to start in the morning and decided to go home.

Working for the service facility was not exactly the most exciting way to spend his day. For the next week, Hylan did what he was told and just accepted that this was the way things would be for the foreseeable future.

He was surprised when he showed up before the long holiday weekend and was summoned into the boss' office. Greg said, "Hey, man! You aced your aptitude and knowledge test. The corporate bigwigs said you got a perfect score."

Hylan was thinking to himself, "So?" What he said was, "That sounds great!"

"Yeah, you're going to be a real up-and-comer, alright. I've already been told to give you an extra 75-cents per hour. After six months on the job, you'll be eligible to go into management training. If you're willing to relocate, you could have your own place to run in the next two years.

Hylan was getting excited. For the first time since he left high school, he had the opportunity to move ahead of the pack because of his smarts and abilities. It might not have been his dream job to work for a car maintenance company. But he could make good money and at least be able to get out on his own sooner rather than later. And, most importantly, he was not going to be working for the likes of Homer!

Everything was going well until his boss, Greg, received his own promotion. Greg packed up his stuff and disappeared without saying a word to anyone. A new guy showed up the next day and took over Greg's office. The name on his uniform shirt said Byron. After calling for a meeting that annoyingly cut into everybody's lunch, Byron introduced himself by saying, I'm Byron The Great! And I will be running this place now. First things first. I want to meet with all of my team leaders to determine just what you are all doing wrong. For the next fifteen minutes, Byron The Great went on and on about how wonderful he was and how we all better tow his line... or else.

It didn't take long for everyone of consequence to hate their new boss.

Two days passed before Hylan had a one-on-one meeting with his new boss. To say that they didn't exactly hit it off would be an understatement. Byron The Great had already read Hylan's file and quickly realized that this kid was either going to be a threat to his job or be leaving to work somewhere else within the company. In no uncertain words, Byron said, "You're going to stay right where you are in supply. We'll see what happens in a few months. I'm not sure if you are a good fit around here." He then told Hylan to go back to work.

Hylan decided right then that this was his last day. His time at Valueline had barely made it into the second month. However, in just two days, his career possibilities within the company had become nil.

Not realizing that he was giving Byron The Great exactly what the arrogant pig wanted, Hylan quit and went home.

He was driving home when his cellphone buzzed. It was Abby! She was training to become a team leader and spent the following few days at a Hooters near Atlanta. She asked if Hylan would like to get together and discuss Kylie's future. Hylan thought about this for a moment and suggested getting their usual room at the Star Light Motel. To his surprise, Abby agreed.

Hylan called his mom to tell her that he would not be home that evening. When he explained why she went into Mom Mode. Hylan's mom explained her concerns and wished him the best. Her words were supportive, but Hylan could tell she wasn't telling him everything she felt. Not wanting to press the issue, Hylan thanked her and disconnected the call.

Abby's arrival was imminent. Giving him little, if any, notice was just like her. Hylan went directly to the motel and booked a room. He made sure it was one with a jacuzzi. He then texted Abby and told her that a keycard was waiting for her in the lobby and that he would meet her there after she finished work.

Hylan was running on a natural high. It felt like old times when he and Abby would get together. He would call her *loblolly*, a pet name for her that he had used for years, and they would fit together like a puzzle piece. There was nothing he needed at home that he couldn't get at a dollar store. He figured that the night would be clothing optional and that little else would matter.

He did have two nagging concerns.

The first and most crucial worry was how they would handle Kylie. He wasn't concerned about her upbringing. Abby was a good mom, or at least he thought so. And Abby's mom would be there to take care of Kylie. Her mom may have been a pushover regarding Homer's will. But Hylan quickly discovered that she stood her ground when it came to Kylie.

Secondarily, Hylan was uneasy about Abby's nightlife.

Hylan was not a partier. His only *release* was an occasional alcoholic drink at the local railroad bar. Abby was into whatever the in-crowd was doing. He knew that she drank a lot of alcohol. But as far as he knew, she was not addicted to anything. However, he would look for signs of abuse while she was here, just in case.

Abby arrived in their room to find Hylan in the bubbling hot tub with the TV blaring. He was facing away from her and did not hear her come in. She dropped her things on the floor and removed her Hooters uniform. It took only seconds for her to be ready to join in.

Hylan was almost asleep. He loved cooking in a hot tub and wished he could somehow control everything in the room without getting out. When Abby dipped her right leg into the water next to him, he was startled. Yet, there were many worse things than having a beautiful, naked woman climb in next to you. Without a word being said between them, they started to kiss.

One thing led to another, and all was forgotten in favor of re-consummating their relationship. Nighttime turned to morning when Abby suddenly realized that she had to get to work. Leaving Hylan in bed, Abby slipped out the door.

Hylan's smile turned to a frown. He suddenly realized that they had barely spoken three sentences together. Nothing had been discussed. In fact, for all he knew, their encounter could result in another unwanted pregnancy.

"Wait a minute," mumbled Hylan to himself. When he was alone, he tended to think out loud. Sitting up in the king-sized bed, he found himself almost in a state of shock. He wanted Kylie. He loved Kylie. The thought that she was unwanted horrified him. Kylie may have been unplanned, but she was wanted and very much loved!

Then he realized his problem. It was Abby he didn't want. She may have been a good mom, but she would always be nothing more than a cheater to him! The evening he confronted her about cheating on him came flooding back into his mind. There was no way he wanted to restart their relationship. He had to have a fresh start!

Trying to figure out an escape plan of sorts, Hylan texted Abby and told her that he would not be available anymore while she was here. He suggested that she find a place to stay on her own. His excuse was that it was too far away for him to be able to get back and forth to work. This all came easy to Hylan since they had never discussed what he was doing for a job or what his schedule might entail.

It felt great to cut her off on his terms. Hylan decided right then that he would find himself some high-paying work. Then, once successful, he would come back to Abby on his terms and tell her how things would be. Yeah! That's what was going to happen.

He took account of his skills, talents, and his ability to make friends and control his enemies. Right there, sitting in the bed, Hylan decided to relax for the rest of the day. He would figure out just what to do with his life.

Climbing out of bed, he turned on the jacuzzi and climbed in. Thinking to himself, he said, "You know what I am good at? I'm really good in bed. How can I make money in bed?"

Well, there was always being a prostitute. But he had no idea how to start. Abby had joked about him becoming a stripper. He had a fabulous physique and was well endowed for his size. He also was extremely flexible because of his years of wrestling. He had been to several strip clubs over the years. Hylan had discovered that when you had a gorgeous woman on your arm and dressed the part, it was easy to get into clubs, even underage.

"Yeah! That's what I'll do," said Hylan to himself. Laying back against the contoured side of the jacuzzi, he stretched out and sighed. "That's what I'll do. And, I know just the club to go to tonight."

PART III.

THE RISE OF JOHNNY RAPID

CHAPTER 10.
TRANSFORMATION

————◆————

Have you ever made a life-changing decision that seemed to release all the pressure, all of the tension built up in your mind? The relief floods through your soul as if the gates of a giant dam are fully opened, allowing the water to pour down the river and swell its banks. And, what does this enjoyment bring? For Hylan, it brought him the best night's sleep… ever!

Hylan had once again transformed into his alter-ego, Johnny Rapid. And Johnny was on a mission.

Most superheroes of legend tend to go after the so-called bad guys. Once defeated, the crusader moves on to fight another heroic battle with little, if any, concern for the vanquished. Could this be why evildoers become supervillains? Johnny decided that rather than fighting evil, maybe the best use of his skills would be to help those closest to him be good.

Other than his mom, Johnny Rapid knew that the most important person in his life was his daughter, Kylie. His current quest would be one of his most important. Johnny would make sure that, no matter what the situation, Kylie would always be able to take command of her life.

Kylie stayed with Abby's parents when her mom traveled. Johnny had two major issues with that. Both involved Abby's parents. First, there was his nemesis, Homer's obnoxious and violent tendencies. The second was the submissive attitude of Homer's wife, Sarah. In many ways, it was Sarah's attitude that bothered Johnny the most.

Johnny's mom was strong-willed and decisive. He wished that Kylie could live under his mom's mentorship. Since this was not to be, Johnny Rapid's quest would be to ensure that Kylie would grow up strong and self-assured.

Johnny Rapid had many abilities far greater than the average person. Unfortunately, one thing that he could not do was fly. Over time, Johnny discovered that one of his skills was to control how long it took to get from one place to another. It was almost as if he could somehow warp time. He wasn't exactly *The Flash* of comic book legend. But he could get from one place to another quickly and be where he needed to be almost instantly.

So, when Johnny decided to visit Kylie, he found himself standing in her bedroom. She cooed quietly while enjoying the deep sleep of a content infant. Looking around the room, Johnny was surprised by its spartan appearance. There were very few toys and almost no clothing for the eye to see. He opened a few drawers and perused the closet. The typical clothes of an infant were available but slim in choice. Johnny walked out of the bedroom and into the living area to find a bassinet and an empty playpen. His first thought was that she went from one form of confinement to another. He would have to make sure that Kylie always had the opportunity to enjoy playtime and the things she needed to learn and grow. "Did Abby live like this when she was a kid?" Johnny thought to himself. Things would have to change! Kylie needed to know that he would be there for her and always be her superhero no matter what the situation.

Walking back into Kylie's room, Johnny Rapid stood over his daughter's crib and stared. Almost as if reciting a prayer, Johnny said, "My dearest Kylie, rest assured. I promise that you will not have to endure the torment and pain I suffered as a kid. You will grow up to be as beautiful as you Mama and as savvy as me. Every opportunity will be available to you. This is my promise to you."

Johnny quietly walked into Homer and Sarah's bedroom. They were both sound asleep with Homer snoring up a storm. The stench of alcohol permeated the room like neglected food left to rot. Staring down on them, Johnny quietly said, "You will not bully my Kylie. You, Homer, will treat her with the respect a new soul deserves and should enjoy. You, Sarah, will stand up for Kylie whenever she needs assistance and love." With that said, Johnny waved his hand over the two sleeping grandparents and walked out of the room. Even in the dark house, anyone watching would have been surprised by the glowing white light emanating from their room. As it faded, Johnny knew that Kylie would be okay.

With that, Johnny Rapid turned and went home. He had a long day ahead of him. Johnny would be looking for a job, a career, that would bring him the success and notoriety he craved.

Johnny Rapid would continue to be a superhero. He would become the best of the best. He would accomplish this because he knew he could.

Almost instantaneously, Johnny Rapid found himself home. The weight of the world lifted from his shoulders. It was time for him to step out into the world and let Johnny Rapid take his first step toward success.

CHAPTER 11.

I THINK I CAN!

————— •··•◆•··• —————

That evening Johnny Rapid went to Hunk-O-Lot in downtown Atlanta. Hunk-O-Lot was a well-established male strip club with a regular clientele. This was a place that tended to ask no questions. The entire goal of the establishment was to make sure that anyone who wanted to ogle the *entertainment* and pay $15 for a drink had a good time.

Johnny had been there before with Abby. The first revelation that came to his mind was Abby's reaction while in the club. After witnessing the way she stared at the performers, he should have realized that she might not just be a one-man girl. On the other hand, it can't hurt to look. Right?

He scanned the room for a moment. Johnny found himself surprised. Considering that he was only 18. No one seemed to care that he was there or bother with him… at all.

No matter what kind of club or restaurant you might be in, finding the people in charge was usually an easy thing to do. But in the case of Hunk-O-Lot, this was turning out not to be true. The club was set up with a myriad of tables scattered haphazardly around a large room. Miniature stages dotted the floorplan with the lighting focused on them. This created odd shadowing made worse by the lack of décor of any kind. As far as Johnny could tell, the walls, ceiling, and floors all seemed to be colored black. Other than the required emergency exit lights, there was nothing on the walls that gave any kind of dimension or direction for the eye to grasp.

Johnny decided that his best course of action was to head for the bar. Besides the manager, one could always count on the bartender to be the most knowledgeable person in the room. Although crowded, Johnny foueasily mades way to an available stool. But rather than sitting, he raised his left hand to signal for service.

"What can I do you for?" asked the barkeep. Standing across the bar from Johnny was a haggard-looking middle-aged man with an impatient expression on his stubbled face.

"Just looking for information," replied Johnny. "I'm looking for work. Can you tell me who to talk to?"

Looking Johnny up and down with skepticism, the bartender said, "You want to talk to Jake? Hold on a sec. I'll buzz him over." Reaching under the bar as if trying to retrieve a gun, he felt for a hidden button. Pushing it, he continued with, "Just take a seat. Jake will be here in a few minutes. But, hey, listen buddy. Let me give you some free advice. Only two kinds of guys work here – Those who can perform and those who take care of the performers. Even our wait staff falls into the second group. You had better keep that in mind if you really want to work here." With that said, the barkeeper moved on to the next person as if Johnny had just plain disappeared.

Johnny knew that he did not cut the profile of your typical bouncer. Even though he knew he could take care of himself, he still had to sell his talents and skills to this Jake person. After what seemed to be an eternity but only added up to about six minutes, a tough-looking dude dressed like a throwback to the 1980s disco era sauntered up and introduced himself.

"What can I do for you?" asked Jake, the club manager. "I'm a busy guy. This had better be worth my time."

"I'm looking for a job," said Johnny. "

"Oh yeah?" retorted Jake in a surly voice. "Okay. Nobody can say I don't give anybody asking a shot. Let's take a walk and discuss your tryout."

Johnny followed Jake away from the bar toward the back of the large room. As they approached, Johnny noticed that there was vertical trim spaced about three feet apart, running up and down the wall. Without any hesitation, Jake raised his hand and walked through a hidden swinging door. Johnny followed him into a small alcove that was lit by what looked like a few white Simontmas tree lights scattered across the trim on the ceiling.   Jake waited for the panel to swing closed behind Johnny. Turning, Jake pushed open another door that led to a brightly lit room that turned out to be the sitting area for the employees. It wasn't exactly a lounge as it was a staging area for the staff.

"Okay, my friend, let's get you into a costume and see what you can do," said Jake. "I'll let you talk with one of my guys so you can get a lay of the land and know what to do."

Confused but thoughtful, Johnny did what he was told. He was introduced to a large man with the stage name of Hunk Doogan. It turned out that all of the performers at the club had the name *Hunk* in their name. Standing at six-foot-three and weighing in at a very muscular 220 pounds, Hunk said, "Hey, good to meet you. Are you a new guy, or do you have some experience?" Turning back to Jake, Johnny was surprised as he realized that Jake had seemingly evaporated into thin air.

With a stern expression, Hunk Doogan said, "You're with me now. Jake will let us know when you can start your tryout. Before that, let me give you some advice. Your job is to impress the women. If the women get excited, they get happy. When they're happy, they drink more. The more they drink, the more they tip. This is all about the women-folk here. Their guys, if they are with any, are in this to get laid. All anybody cares about here is selling drinks and getting lots of tips.

Johnny was starting to get nervous. He said, "I really came here to get a job as a bouncer."

Hunk Doogan guffawed at the thought. He looked at Johnny Rapid with disgust and disdain. "Are you kidding me?" he asked. Not waiting for an answer, Hunk continued, "What are you, about five-foot-six? You look like you're pretty well put together. But, you'll never make it here as a bouncer. You have to be intimidating. If no one has ever told you this before, then let me be the first. You ain't going to scare anyone, anywhere, at any time. Jake told me to get you ready to perform. So, are you up for it or not?"

This is not what Johnny wanted to do. He was extremely nervous about the idea of performing in front of women. Getting up in front of people to protect them is what he knew. In his own mind, he knew Johnny Rapid could do anything. Yet, performing in front of women he didn't know scared him.

"Hey, look man, I'm here to protect people, not dance for them," said Johnny. "I can take on anyone. If Jake would give me a try bouncing, I'd be happy to show him what I can do."

"Forget it, kid," said Hunk Doogan. "You're not going to fit in here." Hunk turned and took a step, then hesitated. Turning back toward Johnny, he said, "I'd scram out of here, kid. If you know what's good for you, I would get the hell out of here while you still can walk out on your own."

Johnny Rapid did not come to Hunk-O-Lot to get into a fight. He knew perfectly well that he could stand his own if the time came. But fighting was not the way to do it here. It was obvious to Johnny that he would not be welcomed as a defender in this place. It was also quite evident that he would have to rethink his options.

Reaching out his hand to Hunk Doogan, Johnny thanked the obnoxious performer and turned to leave the joint. Johnny did not take the time to wait for the doors to close as he sauntered back into the main room of the club. Without realizing it, the bright lights of the backroom acted like a spotlight silhouetting him as if on a stage. For a brief second, all eyes turned to see what was causing the disturbance.

The backlight quickly disappeared, returning the room to darkness. Not seeing anything of importance, everyone's attention returned to the performers except one, as Johnny made his way to the door. A young woman not much older than Johnny came up to him and stuck a dollar bill in his belt. It turned out that she also worked at Hunk-O-Lot and heard about the kid looking for a job.

She said, "Hey, look! You're going to be great. My advice is to find someplace where you can make a difference. You're cute and have a great air about you. Go find a place that's more *you*. With that said, she gave him a quick kiss on the cheek, winked, and turned to walk away.

Speechless, Johnny thought about following her. He took two steps, stopped, then turned around. As Johnny strode to the exit, he said to himself, "She's right! I don't just think I can. I know I can! If this place doesn't want me, I know there are others that will."

Johnny walked into the parking lot with no fear or animosity. He would go home and do some research. "I can do anything I put my mind to," he said to himself. His time at Hunk-O-Lot taught him an important lesson. Johnny Rapid would not perform in front of women. Most of his youth had been spent finding ways to stand up to the bullies in his life. He would find a way to show those that thought he could never be the best that they were wrong. He would finally show those who thought he could not stand up for himself that he could.

The best way to show the bullies of the world that he was their equal or better was to splash his abilities in their faces. Like the fairy tale, <u>The Little Engine that Could</u>, Johnny now knew what to do.

He would find a way to show the world that he could be the best. And that's precisely what he set out to do.

PART IV.
AM I A
SUPERHERO?

CHAPTER 12.
OPPORTUNITY KNOCKS

———————•··•◆•··•———————

Upon his return home, Hylan realized, possibly for the first time in his life, that he was consciously transforming back and forth between two distinct personalities. This revelation did not surprise him as much as realizing that it was a good thing.

"What am I good at?" muttered Hylan to himself. Sitting on the end of his bed, he started to take an account of his strengths, skills, and abilities.

The desire to sleep was gnawing at the back of his mind. As Hylan started to take off his clothes, the dollar bill that had been slipped into his belt floated down to the floor. He reached down, picked it up, and held it up over his head.

Hylan thought about what the waitress said to him.

"Go find a place that's more you," she said.

"What is more me?" asked Hylan to himself.

On the nightstand next to a decrepit lamp that had seen better days was his tablet. He had left it in sleep mode with the Hunk-O-Lot website still sitting on the screen. Laying back onto his pillow and grabbing his computer, Hylan backed out of the site to his original Google search, scrolled down, and found a site offering tryouts for porn performers. *Just call EJ*, the ad highlighted in bold letters.

"Let's see… What am I good at?" asked Hylan to himself. "I'm smart, a good wrestler, and good at sex. But, I could never do porn… could I?"

Thinking about "What would Hylan do?" Then contemplating, "What would Johnny do?" Suddenly, he realized that "Maybe, *Johnny* can do porn!"

So, He made his decision. In the morning, he would call EJ. "After all, it can't hurt to try out, can it?"

••◆••

The next morning Hylan awoke with a newfound enthusiasm. He grabbed a shower and then immediately called EJ from the online ad. After waiting for a callback for several hours, Hylan found himself being pressured by his mom to go out and find a job. His earlier zeal to let his Johnny Rapid persona rule the day ended up being put aside to get her off of his back about work.

That evening, Hylan went to Wild Bill's Country Music and Dance Club and asked if the bouncer position they advertised was still available. The manager looked Hylan up and down with a smirk.

The nightclub was just starting to get busy as the crowd turned to watch the band start their first set. What surprised Hylan was the netting draped in front of the stage designed to stop stray bottles and drink glasses from striking the performers.

Like the club Hylan had visited the night before, Wild Bill's was understaffed and needed additional help. But just like the other evening, Hylan was told that he was too small to be a bouncer. The manager went so far as to laugh at the idea that Hylan could intimidate even a small child.

Hylan felt himself changing. It was the same feeling he had when he morphed into Johnny Rapid in his dreams. He knew that Johnny Rapid and Hylan Taylor were one. But could it really be that easy to move from Hylan, the smart but laid-back kid, to Johnny, his superhero? In that instant, he found out.

"You get your biggest bouncer out here right now!" said Johnny Rapid. "If I can't take him down, then you can throw me out of here!"

Not wanting to make a scene in the club, the manager took Hylan up on his offer but told him that they had to go out back. Turning to lead the way, the arrogant man waved his hand in the air to signal for something out of Johnny's line of sight.

With no fear and excited about the opportunity, Johnny Rapid followed the growing number of club employees through the kitchen and out into the back lot. The area was ringed by a chain-linked fence that seemed to be fighting back against the encroaching bushes pressing against it. Oddly, there didn't seem to be a gate or exit of any kind. It was as if they were now in a pen with the only way out being blocked by the growing audience made up of the staff.

Turning away from the smirking manager, Johnny found himself confronted by the senior bouncer, who had *Bert* stenciled on his shirt. The man had at least eight inches on Johnny and probably outweighed him by at least fifty pounds. But that did not stop Johnny from firmly planting his feet and sizing up his beefy opponent.

"All right, little man. Let's see how you feel about eating some pavement," said Johnny's adversary as Bert sneered at what he thought would be easy prey.

Now, a good wrestler always sizes up his opponent by first looking for which leg he tends to favor. The best first move was to wait for the other guy to make their *first move.*

Johnny Rapid watched as Bert sidestepped and then lunged. It was evident to Johnny that Bert relied on his size and strength to overwhelm and intimidate. The next thing that the audience witnessed was Johnny turning, grabbing the larger man's wrist, and using Bert's momentum to drive him to the ground face first.

Still holding Bert's wrist, Johnny twisted it behind Bert's back, then spun over his body and solidly pinned the defeated bouncer firmly to the pavement.

"Get up, get him!" yelled several in the crowd.

Try as he might, Bert's arm received painful pressure every time he tried to wriggle free. The so-called fight was over almost before it began, with Johnny Rapid shocking a now cheering crowd of fans.

"Fuck this," was all the manager said. The S.O.B. walked back into the club, shoving his way through his own employees and slamming the flimsy door behind him.

Johnny Rapid released Bert and offered his hand to help the larger man up. Bert refused the help but, after a moment, took the proffered hand with a shake and a smile.

"You're tougher than you look," said Bert. "That was a great move." With that and no worse for wear, Bert followed his boss back into the club.

The rest of the staff trailed Bert inside, leaving one person alone to confront Johnny.

"That was quite a performance," said Jake. "I hear you want to be a bouncer. I'll tell you what. Based on what I just saw here, I'll give you a shot. How about $100 per night, Wednesday through Sunday? Your hours will be five o'clock to one a.m."

It turned out that the asshole manager was the *boss* in name only. Jake's dad was the club owner and wanted Jake to be the manager. But Jake's real love was working as a volunteer firefighter, which repeatedly kept him away from the club, especially on weekends.

So, Johnny Rapid took the job. He was now working as a bouncer. And the fringe benefit that he discovered almost immediately was the opportunity to get laid nearly every night!

•••◆•••

Two weeks passed with Johnny Rapid's skills being tested only once. When an altercation broke out that called for the ejection of the perpetrators, Johnny stepped in and did his thing. The two miscreants found themselves not only literally tossed out of the club but also pinned to their aging pickup truck. Johnny quickly found himself accepted as one of the guys. Even the asshole manager had acquiesced to the skills of what he still considered a pintsize bouncer.

But Johnny Rapid still wanted more. Although he enjoyed his new position and the women that came with it, he still believed that this job was just a first step.

The ad that referred to *call EJ* still weighed heavy on Johnny's mind. There had been two voicemails left for him from EJ. The man always seemed to call when Johnny's attention was focused on his work.

Hylan found himself now constantly in his superhero mode as Johnny Rapid. He discovered that any fear he had went away as long as Johnny Rapid was in control.

After his second weekend of work, EJ sat Hylan down to discuss what EJ called "more lucrative opportunities." As Johnny Rapid, the superhero, Hylan was very enthusiastic.

"I have a bukkake looking for a participant," said EJ. "Are you interested?"

Johnny knew what bukkake was but had never participated in one before. As Hylan, he would have rejected the idea. But Johnny Rapid was eager to try. He knew that this could be a giant first step into the world of porn. If he did well in his first bukkake, then other opportunities would open up.

Still curious, Johnny asked, "I know what bukkake is. But, do you know where they got the word from?"

"You're the first person to ask me that," said EJ. "I wondered that myself when I saw my first event. Bukkake is a Japanese word. It roughly means to *splash with liquid*. I guess that's what you would literally be doing." EJ laughed at his own thoughts.

Porn site producers knew that their audience's desires varied as much as the colors in a rainbow. One person's delight might be a turn-off to the next person's passion. A bukkake consisted of men standing in a circle and jerking off onto the face of someone lying on the floor. The real skill involved was being able to get a *hard-on* at will and to be able to *perform* on-demand multiple times over a relatively short period of time.

When Johnny Rapid arrived at the studio, EJ was disappointed with what he saw. However, he had learned from past experience to go with the flow and see what this kid could do. EJ's concern was Johnny's size. He was not physically a big man. But, he was well proportioned and in excellent condition.

EJ knew that everything was relative to performers. Many fans would be very surprised to discover that their favorite actors and performers were below average in height and weight. Producers knew to take this into account by choosing the other cast members in proportion. Size in real life doesn't matter when everybody involved in a production is more diminutive than the primary character.

It turned out that EJ was not only the owner of the agency but also the porn director. He knew what to look for and how to pick his players. To his great surprise, Johnny Rapid outperformed all of the other participants. To EJ's delight, Johnny was able to continue with multiple repeat performances.

Johnny Rapid was obviously nervous when he joined the circle. His confidence rose when he realized that he was much better looking than all of the other participants. He got a hard-on faster than all of the others and was able to maintain it.

"You performed way beyond my expectations, "said EJ. "That is the way to fucking do it! Maybe, I can do something for you."

Johnny Rapid was ecstatic. He was told that he would get $200 per *shot*. Without thinking about it, Johnny Rapid made $600 in what seemed like no time at all! This was an entire week's salary in less time than it took him to drive back and forth to work.

EJ told Johnny to make himself available on a regular basis. "There is a high demand for bukkake scenes with a variety of characters," said EJ. "I can keep you busy if you can get over here when needed."

It turned out that Johnny's night work at the club worked well with the occasional day work doing scenes for EJ. Johnny also discovered something new about himself that would open up the opportunity of his lifetime.

Through one of the women he met at his nightclub gig, Johnny met a guy nicknamed Barker. Johnny and Barker had hit it off and found themselves spending more and more time together. It didn't take long for Johnny to realize that he was attracted to Barker. And to his delight, it turned out that Barker was interested in Johnny, too. They agreed that since they both had *done* all of the available women in the club that maybe it was time to try something different.

Over the next six months, with money rolling in, Johnny found himself working his days for EJ and his nights at the club. In his spare time, he spent almost every available waking moment with Barker.

Although he shared his alter ego as Hylan with Barker, Johnny Rapid was now the dominant personality in his life. It was because of the freedom his newfound relationship offered him that he decided to take the next step. Johnny Rapid would go ahead and try his first porn scene.

PART V.

UNNERVING SUCCESS

CHAPTER 13.
THE BIG STEP

———•··◆··•———

Johnny Rapid's relationship with EJ went from producer to agent in just one day. In the industry, EJ was considered a triple threat. He could do it all. EJ was not only a successful agent but also a director and an excellent cameraman.

When Hylan told EJ that he wanted to do an interactive porn scene, the man was beside himself. For the last several months, EJ was under the impression that Johnny Rapid would only be a one-man show.

Johnny Rapid was fearless.

Hylan Taylor's successful transformation into his alter-ego made his decision-making process easy. If there was a problem, find a solution. When a self-important bully confronts him, take him out. While others waited for their next opportunity to magically appear, Johnny Rapid *made* his next move on his terms, not others.

Johnny Rapid showed up to the audition excited and raring to go.

It took about an hour to meet the other actors, choose the appropriate wardrobe, then discuss what was expected from him during his first scene. The participants were ready, the lighting was dimmed, the stage was set, then… then nothing happened.

"Umm, we're ready to go," said EJ, who was also the director of this shoot. He was wondering what Johnny was waiting for. "This isn't rocket science. Just do your thing."

Johnny stood there staring at his female counterpart and then back at the director. The one thing he was always very good at was not happening. He couldn't get *it* up.

Hylan's past flashed before his eyes. His mind was racing as he realized that his magic belt and colorful costume had ceased to exist in his psyché. For whatever reason, Johnny Rapid has disappeared and left Hylan standing over his co-star, looking like a fool. It was then that he realized that he would never be able to perform scenes with women.

Annoyed at the situation, the EJ sarcastically said, "Would you be happier performing with a man?"

Then, it happened. Hylan's mind filled with how comfortable he had become in his relationship with Barker. As he started to think about the bukkakes and working with other men, he felt the inner strength return that had all but evaporated. Looking down again at his co-star, Johnny Rapid reemerged and shocked EJ by saying, "Yes, exactly! Let's try this again but with that guy over there."

When Hylan arrived at the studio, he met with two other actors, named Tyler and Raphael. They were preparing to do their own series of scenes. All three of them were in the same changing room, making adjustments to their costumes and themselves. It was during this short time that Hylan imagined himself working with one of them. Both men preferred to do gay porn over the other alternatives.

Although there was no discussion about the different genres, Hylan could picture in his mind doing gay porn over straight porn. What he didn't realize was that Johnny Rapid inwardly agreed.

Hylan discovered years earlier that his alter-ego allowed his sub-conscious desires to realize themselves. Many a time, Johnny Rapid, the superhero, had no problem doing things that Hylan would never consider. Hylan stood straight up, turned to EJ, and announced, "If Tyler is up to it, no pun intended, I would like to try this all over shooting a scene with him."

Tyler was beaming from ear to ear. His co-star, Raphael, slapped him on the back and said, "Hey, go for it!"

The frustrated director said, "Alright, alright. These are tryouts anyway." Looking at the barely legal teen crouched on the large recliner, he said, "Okay honey, you're out, for now, and you're in," pointing to Raphael as he stood enthusiastically in the wings of the set.

Johnny Rapid was back and finding himself aroused, knowing that he was going to do a scene with Raphael.

EJ took notice and said, "We'll keep it simple. Here's the scene. You two guys just came back from a night out on the town after just meeting this afternoon. You've fallen head-over-heels for each other and can't wait for the bedroom. You take to this recliner like a cat to catnip and start to *do your thing*. Go for it!"

Johnny and Raphael immediately lost any pretense of not knowing each other, quickly disposed of their clothing, and *went for it*." The totally unrehearsed scene was a spectacular audition. The director was pleasingly surprised at how well Johnny Rapid took to gay porn.

It was as if Johnny had been doing this for years. To the surprise of both EJ and Johnny, it turned out that Johnny Rapid was a natural!

EJ was shocked that things went well. He believed that Johnny Rapid had the right look but was genuinely concerned about whether or not the kid could perform.

As soon as he realized that Johnny Rapid was the real thing, dollar signs started to make his ears ring.

EJ was curious if Johnny Rapid could perform another scene with no intermission. "How do you feel about doing another scene?" asked EJ.

"Let's do it!" said Johnny Rapid.

Raphael was used to the *hurry-up and wait* attitude of many producers in the business. While directors were always gung-ho to move on, producers were looking at the bottom line and wanted to make sure that their ducks were all in line. Unsure, but game to try again, too, he said, "I'm game if you are."

Without a second thought, Johnny said nothing as he took Raphael into his arms.

Take-two went without a hitch as the two actors did their thing for a second time. The performance was flawless in EJ's mind. He already knew that Raphael was good at his job. What happily surprised him was how good Johnny Rapid was.

He had a winner! EJ almost licked his lips as he salivated over the possibilities and money he would make.

Johnny Rapid didn't look back. Within just a matter of hours, Johnny was filming his first video. By day's end, Johnny Rapid had wrapped up his first production.

He really was a natural at this, and it showed. The difference between most porn, whether gay or straight, was believability. It was difficult to find performers who could make an audience believe that the actor was truly emotionally involved with their co-stars. Johnny Rapid had this talent. Not only were his scenes believable, but they also allowed the viewer to believe that Johnny was emotionally involved.

With great glee over his discovery, EJ signed Johnny Rapid to a working contract and immediately forwarded the new star's first video over the number one gay porn site, Men.com.

So, what did this mean for Johnny Rapid? Well, it meant that there was going to be no end to all of the videos that would be created and the stars that would partner with him to extend their own fame.

Over the next year, Johnny Rapid would quickly take his place as one of the most sought-after gay porn stars in the industry.

CHAPTER 14.
I'M IN THE MONEY

———•··◆··•———

The work just kept coming. What seemed like just a few days ago quickly turned into a year of skyrocketing success.

Johnny Rapid was now synonymous with the gay porn industry. Between his innate ability to *perform* at will and his warm personality, the public and his compatriots in the business all fell in love with him.

It wasn't long before the money started to roll in, and travel became the norm. Johnny Rapid found himself becoming a celebrity himself and fawned over by adoring crowds. Johnny loved it. However, in many ways, Hylan was scared out of his mind.

But that was the life of a superhero, wasn't it?

Like Clark Kent of Superman fame, Hylan didn't consider himself a mild-mannered person. He wasn't Bruce Wayne to Batman, either. In fact, Hylan found himself immersed in Johnny Rapid to the point that *Hylan Taylor* functionally no longer existed. "Was this a good thing?" wondered Hylan. "Did it really matter?"

Unconsciously, he chose never to answer this question. Deep down inside, Hylan believed that if he did, the answer might distract him from his success.

Yet, succeed he did. Johnny Rapid went on to make a fortune. The kid from the broken home who had a kid while still in high school could now take care of his life. To make life even better, his family actually supported his road to success. Of course, it helped that, for the first time in his life, he was able to live up to his responsibilities.

Johnny Rapid's personal life saw no limits. He spent time with a variety of people while picking and choosing his intimate affairs. In many ways, it was because of these short-term relationships that he was able to conclude his own sexual preferences.

What surprised Johnny the most was how many stars in the porn business were truly acting. Many participants in gay porn were straight and vice-versa in the straight porn world. Just like in the traditional movie business, many actors were just that, acting.

It came down to learning to become the character you were portraying. Viewers of any sort of entertainment wanted to believe what they were seeing. Johnny Rapid had risen to the top of the profession by giving the audience what they wanted, a good performance.

But that wasn't enough for Hylan Taylor.

He wanted to make amends to himself for the years of torment he endured. Johnny Rapid may have been taking on the world by rocketing to the top. But what was Hylan getting out of it all?

Then, something happened that made Hylan realize that his life had changed. He was no longer the scrawny kid targeted by the so-called in-crowd.

During one of his many guest appearances, Hylan found himself face to face with his old nemesis, Sean Thornton. Sean still towered over Hylan with his hundred-pound weight advantage. Even after Hylan became a successful wrestler, Sean still picked on him. Of all the people to run into, Hylan couldn't believe that this scourge from his youth was now right in front of him.

To Hylan's surprise, a hand was extended, and Sean Thornton offered a smile.

"Hey, Hylan! How are you doing?" asked Sean. "Long time no see."

"Uh, hi," was all Hylan could muster to say.

"Look, man, I'm really sorry about all those things I did to you when we were back in school. I don't know what I was trying to prove by picking fights with you." This was the first time Sean had ever started a conversation with Hylan. Every past encounter had begun with an insult or an accusation.

Taken aback, Hylan suddenly realized that Sean wasn't seeing *Hylan Taylor*. He saw Johnny Rapid, a successful actor and now a major celebrity. Hylan had become Johnny Rapid. Now, in his own mind, Hylan realized that he could close his past as a picked-on wimp and know that even his worst enemies saw him as an equal… But, wait! Maybe, even as a superhero?

"I can't say that it's great to see you, Sean," Hylan was standing taller and in command of the situation. Unconsciously, he found himself reaching down to see if his magic belt was indeed in place and shining brightly. In that instant, he found that Johnny Rapid was now in charge of the situation.

Johnny Rapid extended his own hand and shook the placated bully's ham-like mitt. With a smile creasing the corners of his mouth, Johnny said, "Let bygones be bygones. So, what are you doing here?"

The truce had been drawn. In that instant, the last hostile encounters in Johnny's past had now evaporated. The two rivals talked for several minutes, and then both went on their way.

Johnny held his head high. He almost wanted to jump up and cheer. But that was not to be. He was here to literally show off and be seen. Plus, superheroes didn't jump up and cheer. They just stood there and enjoyed the fan's adulation.

"Okay, well, maybe that was going a bit far," thought Johnny to himself. One step at a time.

However, his situation had changed. Maybe, it was time to take on a bigger mountain to climb. At that moment, Johnny started to think about other performers in his business. Who did he need to challenge to truly become number one? Who was number one? Wait! He was already at the top. After all, there couldn't be a true #1 when all of his performances required at least two others.

So, what would be his next challenge? What was the next step for Johnny Rapid?

Then, the proverbial light bulb blinked on over his head. A sensation was starting to peak on social media. Maybe, it was time for his superhero persona to reach out to an even bigger superhero. A person he could challenge to take the same giant step that made Johnny Rapid a number one success.

PART VI.
JUSTIN BIEBER –
TO DO OR NOT TO DO?

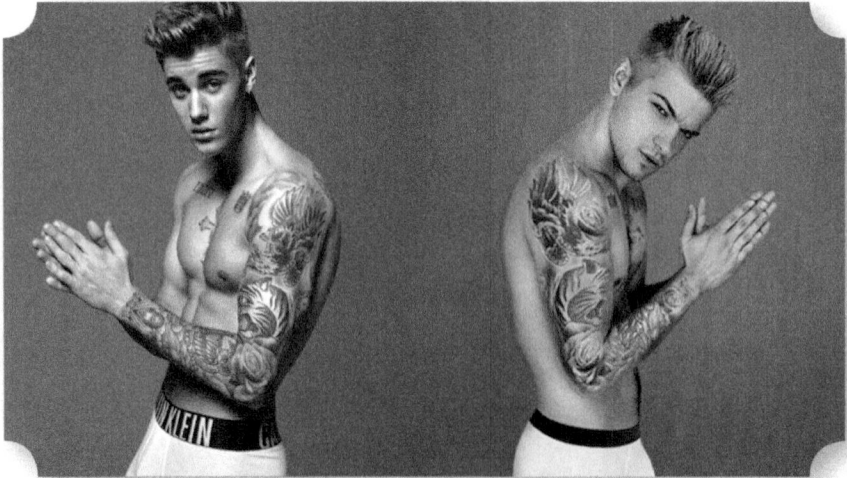

CHAPTER 15.

AN OFFER THAT CAN BE REFUSED

————•··•◆•··•————

The life of a celebrity was rarely their own. Social media guaranteed that any desired privacy was practically forbidden when it came to anyone in the limelight of public success.

Johnny Rapid was no exception. As his popularity rose, it was a foregone conclusion that he had to lay his life out to the public. The challenge was to try to manage the personal exposure and to take care not to do anything that could damage a positive reputation.

Justin Bieber had barely made it into his second decade of life before the unintended controversy of his sexuality became an issue all over social media. His fame and fortune made him a target for writers and photographers looking for controversy. After all, the number of *clicks* to one's website, blog, or podcast could make or break one's success. It didn't necessarily matter what the truth really was. What counted was the news and the questions that could be asked as a result.

Justin Bieber's kissing of Austin Mahone caused a near-cataclysmic social media incident. Was Bieber gay? Was he bisexual? Without even asking the poor guy, assumptions, even absurdities were being made with wild abandon.

Johnny Rapid was not a novice when it came to trying to straighten out his own social media woes. Although he had managed to avoid controversy, he did have to be careful about what he posted and how he handled his presence on the various sites.

On the other hand, why shouldn't he take the big step?

If Justin Bieber was gay or bi-sexual, or even if he wasn't, would he be interested in making a splash in the porn industry?

Johnny wasn't the only person in his sphere of influence to come up with this idea. The management of Men.com, along with his manager, EJ, also thought this was a good move.

Although there was no way to know for sure, Men.com believed they could offer Bieber enough money to take the leap into their business. With this in mind, Men.com immediately turned to their one star, who was about the same age and uncannily looked very much like Justin Bieber. So, EJ asked Johnny if he would approach Justin Bieber for what they thought would be an offer he couldn't refuse.

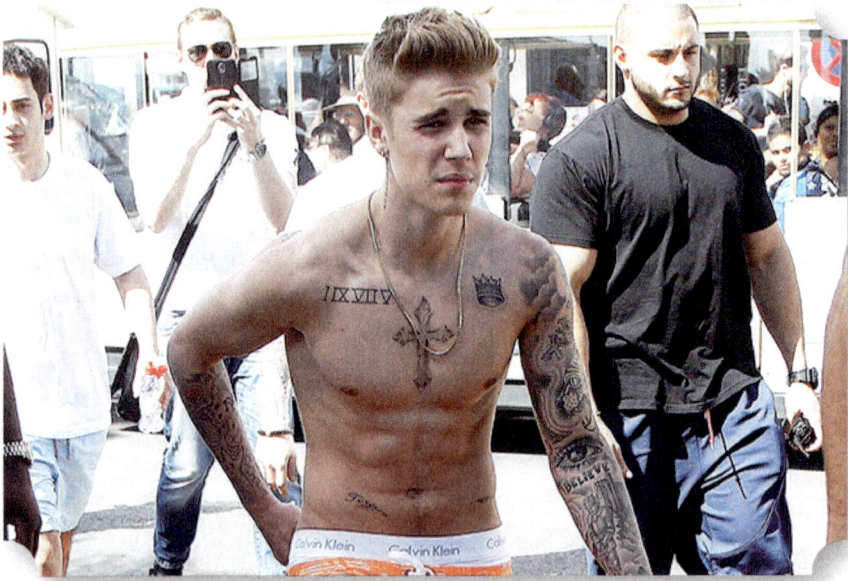

Justin Bieber strolling on the Croisette on day 7 of the 67th Annual
Cannes Film Festival on May 20, 2014 in Cannes, France.
(Photo by Pierre Suu/GC Images) Pierre Suu/GC Images

From Joe Lynch, Editor for Billboard.com

1/15/2015

Gay porn star Johnny Rapid, speaking on behalf of Men.com, is offering Bieber a cool $2 million to film a scene with him.

"I can't even believe I'm gonna say this, but I have an incredible offer for you, Justin Bieber," Rapid said. "Men.com and I are offering you $2 million to do a scene with me. Two million, that's insane! Anyways, it will be easy. I'll do most of the work: come in for a few hours, then you're out of here with $2 million. Hope to see you soon!"

For the record, Johnny Rapid does gay porn but identifies as straight. Although his most popular clips appear to find him on the receiving end, his "I'll do most of the work" comment makes it seem like he's aiming to take the lead on this project.

The offer launched Johnny Rapid's social media presence into the atmosphere. Anyone who knew Justin Bieber quickly learned who Johnny Rapid was and what he was proposing.

For two-million dollars paid by Men.com, Justin Bieber would just have to spend a couple of hours of his time with Johnny Rapid. Men.com believed that this princely sum of money was close to what Bieber was worth at the time. So, by making this offer, they believed that the star singer would leap toward the idea.

Men.com and Johnny Rapid's hopes were raised when there was no immediate response. There was almost a stunned silence as Justin Bieber's followers waited with bated breath for a response from their own superhero.

Although Men.com only offered Johnny Rapid an eighth of what they were willing to pay Bieber, Johnny finally relented due to the massive exposure, no pun intended, he would get from the dramatic publicity. In fact, Johnny's existing videos had quadrupled in views.

But in the end, a private response was sent to Men.com stating that their client, Justin Bieber, was not interested at this time in doing anything other than performing as a singer. Publicly, Justin Bieber said that he was not gay. In fact, his exact comment was derived from his Instagram video in June of 2015, *"I'm not gay but even if I was that's not an insult."*

In Hylan Taylor's mind, this was still a great success. In a way, his superhero had beaten an even greater superhero in his fans' minds. Was Justin Bieber hiding from what he really was deep down? The answer really didn't matter to Johnny Rapid.

Johnny's fame and fortune continued to rise. His popularity rivaled all others in gay porn productions. He had made an offer that *could* be refused. However, in making the offer, Johnny Rapid gained even more notoriety.

"Thank you, Justin," was the thought that ran through Johnny's mind about the incident. "Thank you for helping me realize that my own inner superhero bested the day!"

CHAPTER 16.
THE JUSTIN BIEBER LOOK-ALIKE

+·•·◆·•·+

"So, let's give the public what they want," said EJ to Johnny Rapid.

A smile crossed Johnny's face as he thought about EJ's proposal. The idea of portraying a Justin Bieber lookalike character intrigued him. There would be no direct mention of anyone other than Johnny Rapid. However, it would be quite obvious to those who cared what was going on.

Johnny had always been a fan of Justin Bieber. They were about the same age and with some restyling of his hair, he had an uncanny resemblance to the pop star.

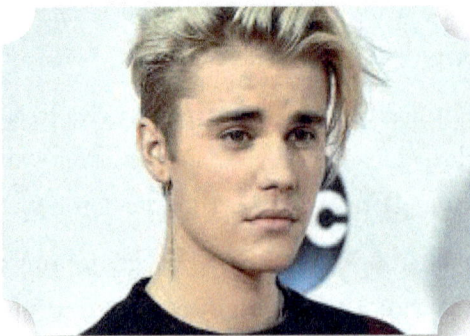

EJ left the office, closed the door behind him, and left Johnny alone.

As Johnny sat back on the couch that had been used for many an *audition* in its past, he started to relax. At times like this, when he was alone, Hylan's emotions emerged.

Hylan knew that Johnny Rapid was an extremely important part of his life. It was because of his alter ego that he found so much success. In many ways, Hylan's self-confidence revolved around his real-life superhero. But it wasn't until that very moment that Hylan realized that maybe everyone had their own superhero deep down in their soul. When push came to shove, did others shift from one version of themselves to another?

Thinking about this, Hylan wondered if Justin Bieber was his own superhero. After all, Justin was just a teenager when he found his success, too. Was his leap into the limelight the result of allowing his inner strength, his *superhero,* to emerge?

Now, Hylan wished he had an opportunity to talk with Justin. They may have more in common than anyone would have believed.

Hylan was intrigued about the next video that EJ was setting up for Johnny Rapid. In some ways, Johnny would take on a role of a superhero who was even greater than Johnny himself.

"Wait," said Hylan to himself. "Is Justin Bieber, the superhero, greater than Johnny Rapid?"

"What is a superhero," contemplated Hylan to himself. "When you get right down to it, a superhero is someone who *saves the day* from others wanting to stop or hurt you in some way. That would make Justin Bieber a more powerful superhero than Johnny Rapid because he affects the lives of more people. Right?"

"But, that's okay!" thought Hylan. "As long as our superpowers are used for good, then that's okay."

At that moment, EJ came back into the office. He said, "We're all ready for the shoot. Why don't you get down to makeup and get your Bieber look on!"

"Won't we get in trouble with me pretending to be Justin Bieber?" asked Hylan.

"You're not going to *portray* Bieber. You're just going to inadvertently *look* like him," said his crafty manager. "After all of the publicity from your two-million-dollar offer, it's not our fault that people read what they want into your next video."

Hylan thought about this for just a couple of seconds before realizing that he would just be doing another porn scene. He was not going to even try to be Justin Bieber. But EJ was right. The chance resemblance between the pop star and the porn star would be a lot of fun to exploit.

Over the next several hours, a fictionalized version of Justin Bieber was filmed. Men.com would have another hit on their hands. And Johnny Rapid would have another feather in his cap.

Hylan's only regret after the day's events was not having the opportunity to meet the real Justin Bieber. After all of the trials and tribulations in Hylan's existence, he believed that bringing his inner superhero into reality in the form of Johnny Rapid saved his life. Hylan wished that he had the chance to ask an even greater superhero if this was a part of his life, too.

PART VII.

THE EXPLOITATION OF JOHNNY RAPID

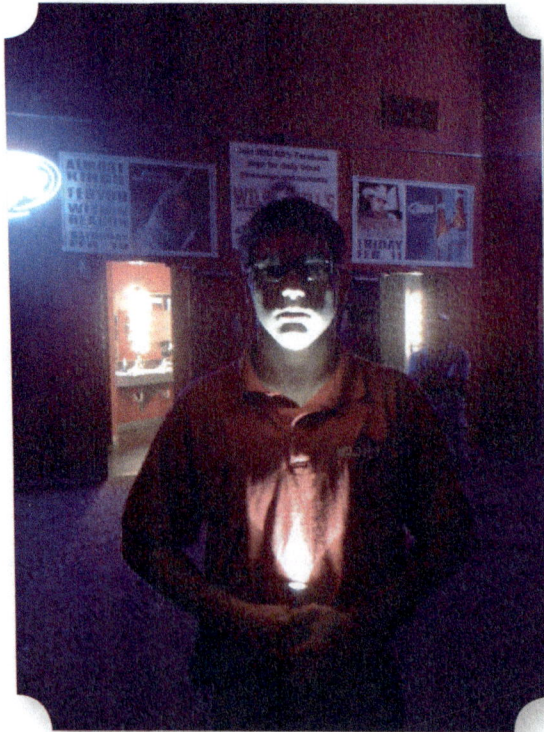

CHAPTER 17.
A GRIM REALIZATION

And life went on for Johnny Rapid.

Moving past the Justin Bieber incident seemed just a part of his career. Johnny Rapid continued to make one successful video after another.

Over time, Johnny Rapid successfully compartmentalized his professional and personal life. In some ways, the two never met. As Hylan, he developed a close group of friends, including his now long-term intimate relationship. This while Johnny Rapid easily found friends among the performers and behind-the-scenes staff that made his videos such as success.

The difference between Johnny and Hylan's companions was just that; they were Johnny and Hylan's. For all intents and purposes, the two groups never met.

As time went by, this worked well for Johnny's career. He tended to party and socialize with Johnny's friends but enjoyed his casual and down times with Hylan.

The irony came into Johnny's situation when it was one of his business acquaintances rather than a friend who warned him about being exploited. During a trip to the Caribbean, Johnny and Cairo were sharing drinks and gossip.

Cairo was from the Middle East. He had immigrated to the United States as a kid when his dad took a job in the Atlanta area. He was actually from Lebanon but quickly discovered that most of the kids in his school didn't know what Lebanon was. So, for better or worse, he just started to say he was from Egypt, thus the nickname Cairo.

Cairo was responsible for a large proportion of the camera work and editing for Johnny's videos. He was considered a wizard when it came to making what was an average shoot look simply amazing when completed. When on location, Cairo and Johnny found themselves hanging out at many of the same venues.

"Hey, look man, you gotta be careful in the future," warned Cairo. "It's real common for you performers to be dumped like yesterday's trash."

Johnny was on his third Long Island Ice Tea and was definitely feeling a bit out of it. It was unusual for Cairo to get all serious on him when they were out partying.

"What do you mean?" asked Johnny.

"Right now, you're number one," said Cairo. "But, that doesn't mean that you are going to stay there. As soon as the next pretty boy steps up, management will push for a change. It starts out with you doing a bunch of videos with you in the lead. Then, after the newbie gets some traction with the fans, you end up with smaller and smaller parts."

Johnny thought about this for a minute. He seemed to always be in demand. It wasn't until this moment that he thought about there being an end to his success.

"But, this is true throughout the media biz," continued Cairo. "What's hot now will be yesterday's news tomorrow. Just take a look at the movie and TV world. Some guy will have great success and end up being sidelined by a younger, prettier dude. You got to take what you can now. You got to go for what you can get now."

The one positive that EJ had explained to Johnny many years earlier was residuals. Although in the beginning, Johnny was making videos to get himself known. He was paid basically for his time. As he became more popular, Men.com agreed to pay a small piece of the profits made from fans viewing his videos, even years after it was made.

Johnny knew that, like himself, Cairo was a contract worker, not an employee. They were both well aware of the turnover in front of and behind the camera. The only sure, long-term job was being in the management of Men.com or as an agent managing performers' careers.

But was he being taken advantage of? Was Johnny Rapid exploited?

When you get right down to it, the answer is *Yes*!

Unlike most businesses, where the majority of employees had defined jobs with specific duties, the movie business was all about each individual project. Performers and production associates were just tools. Obviously, the better the *tool*, the longer it would be used to successfully complete a project.

However, tools wear out, right? Johnny thought about this reality for a moment and tried to figure out if he was being exploited. Was he just being used as some component, some cog in a big machine?

The movie and television businesses were notorious for making the most out of talent and then dumping them as their fan base diminished. Could this happen to him?

"I know you're right," said Johnny, after taking another swig from his drink. "But, what am I supposed to do? I'm actually treated pretty well. I don't feel like I'm being exploited."

"Yeah, well, you say that now," said Cairo. "Just wait until your yesterday's news."

Johnny knew that eventually, he would either be too old or run out of versions of what he was doing to maintain his status among his fans. In a way, he was being exploited. But, he was getting well paid for what he was doing. After all, the gay porn business had made him famous. What else could he have done to achieve this kind of success?

"When you get right down to it, isn't everybody exploited for their skills and talents?" asked Johnny. He had never thought about what he was going to do after his career ended.

"Well, that's just it," said Cairo. "I spend a lot of my time trying to come up with new angles and twists to make our videos stand out. But, there is only so much I can do. You would be surprised, no, maybe you won't, to learn how much nepotism there is in the production side of this business. There's always a job for someone's relative or friend."

"But, that's just it," said Johnny. "You're a standout when it comes to production. You don't have to worry. There is always going to be a job for someone with your abilities."

Johnny continued, "I never really thought about life after porn. But I'm sure something will come up. After all, I can always go back to being a mechanic."

They both smiled at this.

Cairo lifted his drink to toast Johnny. He said, "Here's to hanging on as long as you can. My wish for you is that when you do have to let go that you have a soft landing on something you can really enjoy."

At this point, Hylan's mind pushed past Johnny back into consciousness. He thought to himself about his family. "That's my ultimate future," he mused to himself. He wanted to make sure that he did not make the same mistakes that his parents made. Yes, maybe he was currently being exploited to make others' money. But, for himself, he was going to learn from his life experiences. He would do his best to give his kids the best life possible.

Hylan determined that the exploitation of Johnny Rapid, a superhero, would allow his family to have a great life. And if push came to shove, Johnny Rapid would step up to once again save the day.

CHAPTER 18.
THEY CAN'T HURT ME

———•··◆··•———

That was the amazing thing about having a superhero as an alter ego. Although Hylan could be hurt, Johnny Rapid was invincible.

The next morning after getting a good night's sleep in his hotel room, Hylan contemplated his conversation with Cairo. "Am I being exploited? Well, maybe. Do I care? Ahh, not really.

Johnny Rapid knew what he was getting into that night when he decided to take EJ up to participate in a Bukkake. Ever since then, everything he did was by choice. There was no one forcing him to do anything. In fact, it was Johnny Rapid who stepped up and created new ideas for the gay porn entertainment world.

His fans loved him. At least, that's what constantly appeared on his social media. If there were any complaints, they were mostly centered around wanting more!

All-expense paid travel, an expense account when on the road, and an adoring audience wherever he went. He wanted for nothing.

And, the best part?

Well, the best part, maybe the most important part, was relaxing when he did go home. He was comfortable enough with his life and himself that he could put his superhero belt away in favor of enjoying his loving family and friends.

"So, if this was exploitation, then give me more," said Johnny. "The worst thing that could ever happen to me is to get physically hurt. Fortunately, there's nothing in my performances that would lead to injury. As long as I can perform, as long as my fans want me out there, I, Johnny Rapid, will be there!"

With that cheerful thought and a smile on his face, Johnny Rapid left for the airport to go home.

"They can't hurt me!" said Hylan out loud. "Johnny Rapid will not let them!"

PART VIII.

LOOKING BACK SOMETIMES, IT HURTS

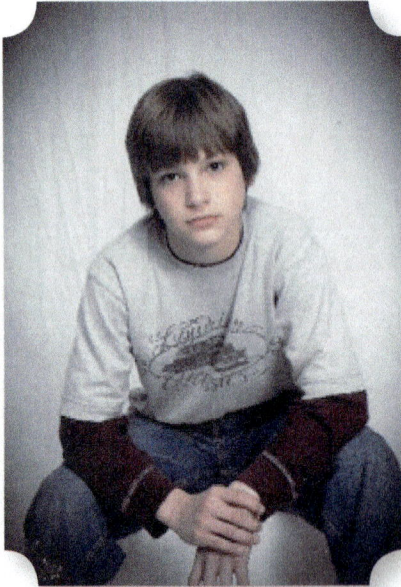

CHAPTER 19.

WHY BE HYLAN, BE JOHNNY

———•··◆··•———

When traveling to Atlanta, Georgia, from almost anywhere in the world, one usually finds themself on Delta Airlines. Also, it really makes the choice simple when the airline automatically upgrades you to first-class whenever you travel.

Reclined in a seat that made royal thrones seem shabby, Hylan found himself daydreaming about his past. "What a night and day difference between life before and after my first dream about my magic belt," contemplated Hylan.

So much had happened since his days in elementary school when he was picked on and sometimes tortured just because he was different. Who would have thought that being smart could become a curse? His school life was miserable back then. And, life at home wasn't much better. Hylan wasn't sure how he would have made it if it wasn't for his dreams.

Then came Johnny Rapid, superhero. No longer was going to school a miserable experience. But, his tribulations led to a chance meeting with a man who became his mentor. Hylan found solace in wrestling. It didn't take long for his confidence to build, his grades to skyrocket, and his loneliness to fade. In less than a year, Hylan overcame his bullied childhood and became the most popular person in school. And it was all because of Johnny Rapid.

Deep down, Hylan knew that Johnny Rapid was an overt version of himself. After all, Johnny was a fabrication from his dreams. The magic belt that gave him his superpowers was all in his imagination, right?

He did sometimes worry that he was living two lives. But, everything he was today was because of the events from his past. If it wasn't for being picked on in school, the breakup of his family, and the unexpected gift of his daughter, Kylie, at such a young age, Hylan would not have worked so hard to make the changes in his life to become so successful.

When you come right down to it, many of us have an inner *Johnny Rapid* that we fall back upon to help us remain strong. If you think about it, there really is a difference between you, *the public person*, and you, *the private soul*. We all strive to separate our public life from what we enjoy at home and with our families.

The more popular you are, the more famous you become. This fact of life creates a need for attempting to separate your public persona from one's private time. The challenge is figuring out how to balance the two without sacrificing your very soul.

Johnny Rapid allows Hylan Taylor to successfully make this all-important balance work in his day-to-day existence. The life lessons from his time in high school, when Johnny Rapid first made his appearance, allowed Hylan to later become number one in a field he would never have thought to pursue.

Thinking about what life was like before he started wrestling, Hylan couldn't imagine being any kind of a public performer. He realized that taking even bad situations and choosing to learn from them rather than running from them made all the difference.

Hylan knew that no matter what the future brought, he would be able to build on his past and stay successful. He also believed that his friends and family would always be there to make his home a loving refuge.

However, his memories sometimes haunted him. He may have learned from his mistakes and the cruelty reaped upon him like a bad-luck hand in a high-stakes card game. But what about the people hurt along the way? He may be living the good life today. Yet, why did it hurt so much when most of his past was not his fault?

Guilt is a strange bedfellow. "Have you ever noticed that it only seems to rear its ugly head when you are alone, trying to get some sleep?" mumbled Hylan to himself. He glanced at the passenger next to him to make sure that he wasn't talking out loud. Even in the luxury of first-class, he still had someone sitting close by. The good news for him was the quiet snoring emanating from his nearby seatmate.

"Why am I feeling sorry for myself?" asked Hylan to no one in particular. "I have a great family, my career is going well, and my friends are tried and true. Yet, yet… Sometimes, I still hurt."

Sleep always seemed to come easily to Hylan. Closing his eyes, he fell asleep. The jet plane's quiet roar slipped away. He found himself figuratively tightening his magic belt. And once again, his superhero, Johnny Rapid, stepped up to take away his hurt and save the day.

As his subconscious mind took over, Johnny Rapid started to play clean-up hitter, like the baseball batter fourth in line to bring any runners on base home. Johnny Rapid may have been the turning point in Hylan's past. But, he was also Hylan's greatest supporter in the present. What Johnny could not accomplish by day, he made sure got done in Hylan's mind by night. In almost all of the ways that count, Johnny took Hylan's past and made it work for his future.

Whether consciously or not, Hylan not only took care to understand his past but also learned how to enjoy his future.

PART IX.
JOHNNY RAPID INDEED IS MY SUPERHERO

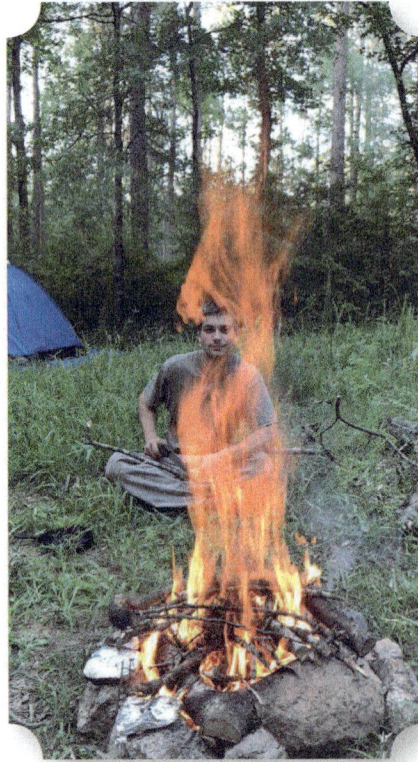

CHAPTER 20.
ADVENTURES

———•··◆··•———

Indeed, you won't be surprised to hear that when Hylan thinks about the most enjoyable moments in his life, they tend to revolve around the adventures of Johnny Rapid.

Sure, we can talk about intimate relationships, vacations, and even a great meal with friends. But, almost everything in life takes a second chair to one's own superhero. It may be hard to admit it. Everyone has an inner superhero. When it comes to a difficult job or task that must be accomplished, we all reach deep down into our inner beings for that extra help.

In Hylan's case, Johnny Rapid became a *real* superhero. Not only did his family watch him step up and begin to achieve, but his friends, and yes, even his enemies, discovered that he was a force to be reckoned with.

The amazing thing is that Hylan's closest friends are truly unaware of all of the things Johnny Rapid has done. Whether it's his popularity, career, physical condition, self-defense, or even making love, Johnny Rapid is either the best or damn close to it.

At not even thirty years of age, Johnny has traveled all over the world, hung out with the elite of society, gone on high adventure expeditions that would terrify many, and almost *never* turned down a challenge unless it affected others in a bad way.

Yet, in so many ways, Johnny's greatest accomplishment is the freeing of Hylan Taylor's soul. Today, Hylan now knows that he is in control of his life. Whether he has been *exploited* or simply *used*, he voluntarily went along for the ride. And, regrets? Well… There are very few.

We all have things we might have changed in our lives if we could go back in time. In Hylan's case, he knows that his past adventures have made him strong. He can take whatever life throws at him and hit a proverbial home run.

And what in Hylan's mind is his greatest accomplishment, his greatest adventure? Simply… Fatherhood. With the recent birth of his second child, he now finds himself in a place in life where he can take care of his cherished gift. Is he putting aside his adventures?

"Absolutely not!" is Hylan's retort. "Life is one long adventure! I'm just glad that I am in a position to give my undivided attention to my family without too much worry about what is ahead."

And that's the great thing about being Hylan Taylor. He knows that Johnny Rapid can step up at any time to be there when needed.

The difference between Johnny Rapid, Hylan's superhero, and many of us out there in the world is the admission that we all have a superhero deep down inside of us. It took the abuse and misery of his childhood to bring out Hylan's alter ego.

What does he ask all of us? Simply, "Why are you waiting? What is it going to take for you to release your superhero?"

•••◆•••

Printed in Great Britain
by Amazon